Stop Pr(

A Simple Guide to Hacking Laziness, Building Self-Discipline, and Overcoming Procrastination

Nils Salzgeber
www.njlifehacks.com

Copyright © 2017 Nils Salzgeber

This eBook is licensed for your personal enjoyment only. This eBook may not be re-sold or given away to other people. If you would like to share this book with another person, please purchase an additional copy for each recipient. If you're reading this book and did not purchase it, or it was not purchased for your use only, then please return to wherever you obtained it and purchase your own copy. Thank you for respecting the hard work of this author.

Disclaimer

Please note that this book is for entertainment purposes only. The views expressed are those of the author alone, and should not be taken as expert instruction or commands. The reader is responsible for his or her actions.

Download The Action Guide FREE!

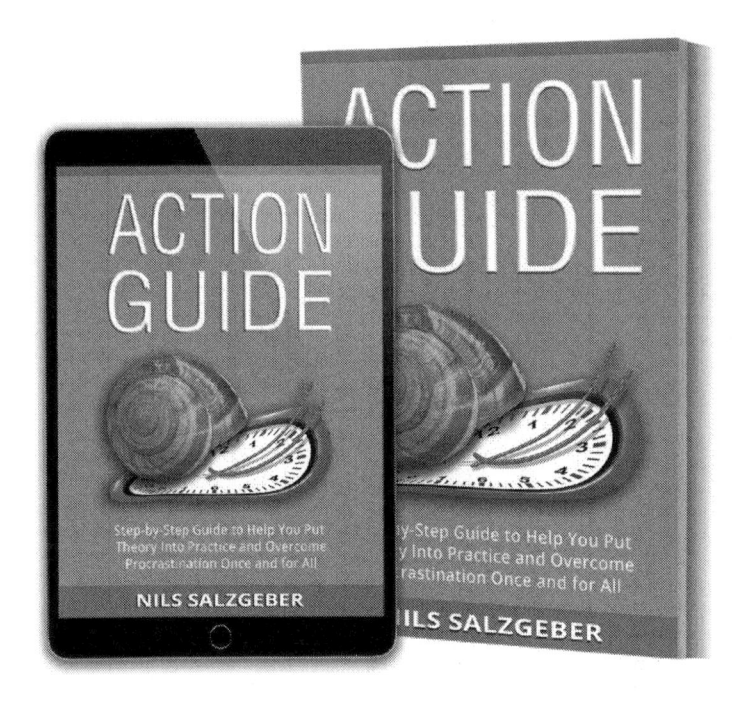

READ THIS FIRST

You'll have the most success in overcoming procrastination when you actually apply the tactics from the book. The Action Guide takes you by the hand and shows you how to do that step-by-step.

Just to say thanks for downloading my book, I'd like to give you the Action Guide 100% FREE!

To download, go to: njlifehacks.com/lp/procrastination-action-guide/

Contents

Introduction	5
"This Needs to Stop"	8
How This Book Is Organized	11
Chapter 1: Know Thy Enemy	13
Chapter 2: Awareness	19
Chapter 3: The Paradox of Getting Started	26
Chapter 4: What Productivity Gurus Won't Tell You About Procrastination	38
Chapter 5: The Magic of a Simple Plan	45
Chapter 6: Carrots & Sticks	52
Chapter 7: Why Your Granny Doesn't Procrastinate	58
Chapter 8: The Power of Nice	67
Chapter 9: The Art of Emotion Surfing	76
Chapter 10: The Science of Willpower	87
Final Thoughts	105
About the Author	109

Introduction

Let me guess: You're the kind of person who sincerely wants to become more productive and disciplined, exercise regularly, eat healthy, wake up early, and finish tasks and projects on time.

But for whatever reason, you just can't seem to make these things happen. You struggle to follow through on your goals by successfully putting your intentions into practice. Paradoxically, you're unable to force yourself to do the very things you're sure you *want* to do.

Certain activities, for reasons you don't understand, feel too uncomfortable to pursue — indeed, you shudder just thinking about them. And so you end up wasting massive amounts of time watching TV, playing video games, dillydallying on social media, or otherwise distracting yourself.

Then once you snap out of your distraction, you feel terribly guilty about how you've spent the last couple of hours. You respond by harshly criticizing yourself, which further adds to your misery and causes you to drown yourself in even more distractions.

Does this sound anything like you? Good! You're in the right place. You're a procrastinator, and you're here because you're looking for a solution to end your struggles. You're here because procrastination is causing massive pain in your life and you've about had enough.

Maybe it's the constant guilt that's suffocating you. Maybe it's the building stress or anxiety. Maybe it's the relentless self-criticism. Or maybe it's the never-ending background feelings of misery, disappointment, and unhappiness that are weighing you down.

These sensations of shame, disappointment, and lack of fulfillment lead you to question whether you'll ever be truly happy, especially since you know deep inside that you're wasting your potential day in and day out.

The funny thing about procrastinators is that they know how capable they truly are — how much potential they have to make meaningful and transformative changes to their lives — even as they continue to struggle with transitioning from *thinking* to *doing*. You know what you've got inside you. You know you could achieve great feats in life and make big things happen. Armed with this self-knowledge and insight, the fact that you can't seem to actually make those positive changes damages your self-esteem and detracts from your happiness.

Consequently, the procrastinator's life tends to be characterized by missed opportunities, wasted potential, fear, shame, guilt, and disappointment.

And if you think things are bad right now, consider all your future regrets of not living up to your potential, putting forth enough effort, or even caring adequately for your mental and/or physical well-being. You're likely to experience significant pain and disappointment that won't dissipate until you get a handle on the situation

Procrastination is sometimes called "the thief of time." But it's much more than that, isn't it? Not only is it the thief of time, but it's also the perpetrator of evil, the killer of dreams, and the creator of endless problems.

And if you're reading this book, you probably already know all that. You're perfectly familiar with all the negative consequences of procrastination, aren't you? Heck, you're probably procrastinating right now by reading this book instead of doing something you know you should be doing, but is too uncomfortable to pursue.

If procrastination is such a painful condition, why don't we stop doing it? Why can't we just do the things we know we need to get done? Why do we keep delaying action? And what can we do to break free of procrastination's grip and finally get some real work done?

If you're interested in the answers to these questions, you're probably in a situation similar to the one in which I spent most of my life. Up until two years ago, I was the worst procrastinator imaginable. I had zero self-discipline. I couldn't get anything done without being subjected to significant outside pressure. And I was suffering the consequences living as a procrastinator day in and day out.

Since that time, I've gone through a remarkable transformation, which I'm going to use to teach you which specific tools and tactics you can use to finally overcome your tendency to procrastinate. This book presents a concise, yet detailed summary of the key lessons I've learned over the last few years fighting my own battles against procrastination. You're going to learn exactly how procrastination works, why you do it, and why you can't seem to stop. Most importantly, you're going to discover the most potent tools to stop delaying and start getting things done.

These strategies will work for you whether you're a failing student, a successful business person, a stay-at-home mom, an aspiring entrepreneur, or a "lost cause" with little hope of improvement.

I promise that if you follow the tactics outlined in this book, you'll immediately experience a significant decline in your day-to-day procrastination. You'll be able to start on tasks earlier, get things done on time, and feel a whole lot better about yourself in the process.

Will this book completely eliminate your tendency to procrastinate? Of course not. What you can expect, however, is to procrastinate a lot less. Even better, you'll no longer feel so terribly guilty about it, beat yourself up over it, or get super stressed about it. And as an additional bonus, you'll be able to enjoy your leisure time without constantly feeling like you should be working.

Sound fair? Let's get to it!

"This Needs to Stop"

A little over two years ago, I moved out of my parents' home and into a new apartment with my brother Jonas.

I had just quit university to give this online marketing thing a real shot (I'd started doing internet marketing a few years back and was earning enough to live comfortably). My brother, with whom I'm running a website called NJlifehacks.com, was working part-time in a fitness center. He would often work late shifts and get home after 10 p.m., which meant I spent a fair amount of time alone in the apartment.

It was during that time that I became truly aware of the pain procrastination was causing me. Usually when we procrastinate, we don't realize the extent to which guilt, anxiety, frustration, and other negative emotions are bubbling up inside of us. Most of us just keep distracting ourselves to numb those uncomfortable feelings. But if you're all by yourself, things look different.

For starters, there was the anxiety and resistance I felt when facing certain tasks. I'd get up in the morning with a clear plan to perform my morning ritual and then start working on my business. Even just following through with my morning ritual was ridiculously hard. For whatever reason, I could barely get myself to meditate for 10 minutes — it felt so, for lack of a better word, uncomfortable.

If I was lucky, I'd manage to follow through with the morning ritual, but then the hard part was still ahead of me. Now I had to start writing articles or do some other dreaded task for the business. I felt so much resistance I can't even describe it.

Sometimes I managed to follow through with my plans and sometimes I didn't. No matter what, it was always super challenging. And if I didn't do what needed to get done? OMG, that's when it got really bad. Because that's when the guilt and harsh self-criticism kicked in.

You see, when I couldn't get myself to do what I had intended to do, I distracted myself by watching TV, playing video games, or watching some dumb YouTube videos. During the distraction itself, I felt okay. But the moment I turned off the TV, laptop, smartphone, or whatever... I was in for a real mental beating.

"Why can't I get this right? Why can't I just sit down and do the things I should do? Why am I so terrible at this? Why am I so unproductive? And undisciplined? Why? Why? Why?!"

It was ugly.

And so there I was, drowning in a cocktail of guilt, fear, frustration, and despair. I knew exactly how it worked. If I did the things I was supposed to do, I felt good and everything was fine. But if I didn't find the strength to do these things, I ended up feeling guilty, disappointed, and like a complete failure.

Was I supposed to live like this for the rest of my life — constantly in fear of what would happen if I procrastinated? Constantly engaged in a battle of *wanting* to do the right thing, but being pulled in all kinds of other directions?

If you're a chronic procrastinator, you probably know exactly how that feels. Needless to say, this was one of the hardest periods of my life. Sometimes it got so bad that I was literally crying in my bed, not knowing if I would ever get a handle on this.

The good news is that I indeed got a handle on this, otherwise you wouldn't be reading this book right now.

So, what happened? Pretty soon after moving into the new apartment, I came to a point when enough was enough and I said to myself, "This needs to stop. I am tired of this bullshit. I will figure out this procrastination thing, even if I go crazy doing it!"

I ordered a bunch of books on procrastination from Amazon and began my path of recovery. Over the course of a couple of months, I read and implemented information from many of them: *Eat That*

Frog, The Procrastination Equation, Solving The Procrastination Puzzle, Getting Things Done, The Now Habit, and so on.

Slowly, I started implementing, developing, and refining the strategies you're about to learn in this book. I experienced lots of setbacks along the way, but today I'm at a point I could never have imagined a year or two ago.

I can easily get up early every morning. I take cold showers, meditate, and exercise every day. I can get things done whether I feel like it or not. I feel like I'm calling the shots. I feel powerful, and most importantly, I feel like I'm in full control of my life.

Don't get me wrong, I still procrastinate at times, and sometimes I'm still lazy, and other times, I feel like garbage. But it's not nearly as bad anymore. I don't experience the crazy amount of guilt, anxiety, fear, or despair the way I used to. It's all much more manageable.

Now, why am I telling you all of this?

I want to show you that it's possible to overcome procrastination. No matter where you are right now, no matter how hopeless you feel, no matter how crazy your level of procrastination is, there is a way to get better at this. There *is* a way to procrastinate less, get more things done, and feel in control of your life.

And that is what you'll learn in this book.

How This Book Is Organized

First of all, I've tried to keep this book as short as possible.

The last thing I want is to put a gigantic and overwhelming book into the hands of a procrastinator. It's like handing a loaded gun to a suicidal person — it's just not the right thing to do. With that being said, I feel I've only succeeded partially with this goal. The book came out longer than I hoped, though I'll let you be the judge of that.

Another thing I wanted to do with the book was to provide a good mix between theory and practical strategies.

The theory is useful because merely knowing how something works is oftentimes enough to facilitate change. E.g., once you know that fruit juices are as unhealthy as soft drinks, it's easy to make the change to stop consuming them (assuming you care about your health).

As far as the practical strategies go, I've tried to include as many as possible while still keeping things short. I did this for the simple reason that what works for one person might not work for another. Please don't feel like you need to make use of all the strategies. Pick what you find useful and leave out the rest.

Since most chapters are a mix of theory and strategies, I've put the prefix "TRY THIS" in front of the practical interventions. This helps to better separate the two and makes the information more easily absorbable.

One last thing I want to address is that I've repeated certain ideas throughout the book. This isn't to bore you; rather, it's to help you learn these ideas by heart. As you've probably heard thousands of times in school, repetition is the mother of learning.

The book is roughly divided into three parts.

Chapter 1 is meant to give you an overview of procrastination. It's all about how procrastination works and describes why so many of us fall prey to this dreadful habit. It will help you better understand your own behavior and explain why you act the way you do. Understanding the basics of procrastination can in and of itself be incredibly helpful in facilitating change.

Chapters 2-9 will each explain a key topic regarding procrastination. Each chapter will give you some theory and one or more specific strategies that you can start implementing and reaping rewards from immediately. At the end of these chapters, as well as at the end of chapter 10, you'll find a short summary in which the main point is restated and the aforementioned tactics listed.

Chapter 10 is all about the science of willpower. Because procrastination is ultimately a willpower issue, it makes sense to dive deeper into this topic. The practical interventions presented in this chapter are somewhat different from the strategies in chapters 2-9. They are long-term strategies. Not Band-Aids, but cures. Seemingly ineffective in the beginning, once applied for a while, their compounding benefits will make all the difference in the world.

Lastly, if any questions come up as you're reading through the book, feel free to shoot me an email at nils@njlifehacks.com. I'll get back to you as soon as possible. And now, let's get started!

Chapter 1

Know Thy Enemy — How Procrastination Works and Why You Can't Stop

What exactly is procrastination, anyway?

How does it work?

Why do we do it?

The first question is the easiest to answer, so we won't spend a lot of time with it. Procrastination is the act of delaying or putting off something that should be done. The crucial ingredient in procrastination is that the delay is irrational. We know delaying a specific task isn't good for us, but we do it anyway.

The harder question to answer is why we do it. Why do we put off doing something that would obviously be in our best interest?

Why do we put off exercising when it's obviously good for us? Why do we delay studying when it's obviously what we should be doing? Why do we put off doing the taxes until we get multiple warnings and need to pay a fine?

(Hint: It's because there's a part of us that does *not* want to do these things.)

I've struggled a lot with how to best answer this question. For this book, I've come up with an analogy that I believe makes sense. I've actually stolen it from Tim Urban's TED Talk — credit where credit is due.

The analogy may sound weird in the beginning, but bear with me. At the end of this chapter, it will all make sense and you'll hopefully be able to recognize your own behavior in what I'm describing here. And don't worry if you can't fully identify with the analogy or my overall explanation. The upcoming chapters will provide countless strategies that will work for you, whether you agree with my explanation or not.

With that being said, let's get into it.

According to our little analogy, the reason you procrastinate is because there's a monkey running the show in your brain.

It's not a real monkey, of course.

It's more like a second personality of yours — a personality that resembles the behavior of a monkey.

This monkey operates on the basic guiding principle: avoid what feels bad, approach what feels good. Its primary aim is to feel good right now and to maximize immediate gratification.

The trouble occurs when what *you* (the rational part of you) want to do doesn't line up with what the monkey wants to do.

You want to study for an upcoming exam, meditate, exercise, or work on an important project. The monkey, however, has no interest in doing these things. None of them sound remotely fun or enjoyable. Heck, they sound boring, hard, and effortful — not exactly what a pleasure-seeking creature is looking for.

And so, if you think about doing any of these hard things, the monkey starts revolting.

"Let's watch TV instead," it will say. "You can study tomorrow!" "Meditation is for monks. Don't kid yourself." "You'll feel more like doing it later." "Eat something first. You need some energy."

You're faced with a decision between what you want and what the monkey wants, between immediate gratification and long-term success.

If you listen to the monkey, that's called procrastination. You put off doing what's best for you for something that feels better in the present.

If you don't listen to the monkey, that's an act of willpower. You use the strength of your will to veto the monkey. You forego the pleasures of the moment for potential benefits in the future.

That's procrastination in a nutshell — a battle of impulse versus willpower, emotion versus reason, automatic versus controlled, experiential versus rational, and short-term pleasure versus long-term happiness.

It's a battle between your rational self and your monkey self, between the part of you who wants to be healthy and the part of you who wants to eat candy all day long.

If you're a procrastinator, it simply means you're losing this battle too often.

It means your monkey is in charge most of the time, guiding your behavior away from what feels bad and toward something that makes you feel good in the moment.

The good news is you'll learn exactly how to win this battle more often in this book.

But first, let's dive a little deeper into how procrastination works.

When Emotions Get in Your Way

Procrastination has everything to do with emotions.

Think about the last time you delayed something that you knew needed to get done. Did you experience any of the following thoughts running through your mind?

- "I don't feel like it."

- "I'll feel more like doing it tomorrow."

- "I really don't want to do this right now."

- "I'm just not in the right mood."

This resistance is coming from the monkey's desire to avoid what feels bad, and to avoid negative emotions.

The tasks you procrastinate on always inspire negative feelings in you — dread, anxiety, frustration, boredom, and annoyance. Every time you experience negative feelings, the monkey shows up, urging you to mitigate these feelings.

And what's an easy way to mitigate these feelings? Just put off the task.

Phew, what a relief! Now that you're not faced with the unpleasant task, you feel better.

But for how long? This relief, as I'm sure you know, is usually short-lived. Sooner or later, any initial act of procrastination comes back to haunt you.

A great example of this is what I call the classic *procrastination-guilt-procrastination loop*. You don't feel like doing the thing you should be doing and, in the hope of improving your mood, decide to engage in something more fun. You check your email, scroll through your Facebook feed, maybe watch some YouTube videos. 30 minutes later, you realize you've been procrastinating for no good reason. Worse yet, you still don't feel like doing the thing. And on top of that, you feel guilty for having wasted so much time. Now you're experiencing even more negative emotions and your mood is even worse than it was in the beginning. This means you feel an even stronger urge to run away, making it ever more likely that you'll keep procrastinating.

In short, the initial act of procrastination leads to guilt (and other negative emotions like disappointment and shame), which leads to more procrastination, which makes you feel even worse, which leads to even more procrastination, and so on.

Once you're in that loop, it's incredibly hard to get out. (Believe me, I should know. I literally spent days and weeks in that loop, unable to get out.)

Not only is the task you're trying to accomplish associated with negative emotions, but the initial act of delay piles even more negative emotions on top of those, making the monkey increasingly irritated. In that state, it's almost impossible to resist the monkey's pull away from the uncomfortable feelings and toward immediate gratification and short-term mood repair.

That's another way of defining procrastination: as a short-term mood repair strategy. We can't handle our negative emotions and give in to feeling good. And while this works in the short-term, it makes things 10x worse in the long-term.

If we want any chance of overcoming procrastination, we need to get better at handling our emotions and impulses. Many strategies in this book will help you do so.

Before we get to the actual strategies, however, there's one last thing I want to address…

Are Procrastinators Just Lazy?

For most of my life, I was the kind of guy who bragged about my procrastination.

At university, for example, I could never get myself to study until about two weeks before exams — I just couldn't stop procrastinating. But that's not what I was telling my friends. Instead, the reason I gave them was that I just didn't care. I portrayed myself as the cool kid who just didn't give a fuck about anything.

It's this type of behavior that makes people think procrastinators are just lazy and careless when in fact, the opposite is true: procrastinators care way too much.

Procrastinators, whether they are aware of it or not, are constantly worrying that...

    ...what they do isn't good enough
    ...people will "find out the truth" about them
    ...people will find out that they aren't as competent as believed
    ...they might get ridiculed
    ...they are inadequate
    ...and so on

Procrastination usually stems from some form of fear — fear of failure, fear of success, fear of the unknown, fear of judgment, fear of disapproval.

It's much easier to procrastinate than it is to write a book and risk that people might not like it. It's much easier to procrastinate than it is to start a business and risk failing.

Whatever the exact patterns are, procrastinators tend to worry a lot. They experience more negative emotions when facing certain tasks than "normal" people. As a result, they also need more willpower and better emotion regulation skills than normal people do.

Unfortunately, most procrastinators never learn any willpower or emotion regulation skills. The only coping mechanism most of us develop is procrastination: just put off the task; this will mitigate the negative feelings for a while.

After using this strategy for a while, procrastination becomes a habit. And habits are hard to break.

So, most procrastinators aren't lazy or careless. They have deep emotional issues that require strong willpower and well-developed emotion regulation skills — two things that the average procrastinator doesn't have.

Now, here's the thing: I don't know how to solve these emotional issues for you, and we're not going to dive deeper into these issues in this book. Instead, we're going to learn how to act and get things done in spite of those issues.

That's what worked for me, and I'm positive it'll work for you.

Let's get to it!

Chapter 2

Awareness — The First Step Toward Change and Why You're Ahead of 99 Percent of Your Fellow Procrastinators

The first step toward any serious and lasting change is awareness.

Without awareness, change is at best luck-based or incidental. Think about it: If you're not *aware* of what's going wrong in your life, how are you going to fix it? If you don't realize how, when, where, and why you procrastinate, how are you going to prevent it?

Without awareness, you wouldn't be reading this book.

After all, you wouldn't be *aware* of the fact that you're a procrastinator, and you certainly wouldn't be *aware* of the fact that procrastination is a serious problem you need to be working on.

So, kudos to you. Unlike most of your fellow procrastinators, who have no clue what's going on in their lives, you've already realized that this is an aspect of yourself that you need to be working on.

Even better, you took action toward fixing this issue by buying and reading this book. And who knows what else you've tried before?

The sad truth is that 99% of people out there will never even realize that they procrastinate, let alone take the necessary steps to overcome it.

You're already way ahead of the game.

And if you keep reading and start implementing the strategies in this book, you'll slowly but surely weaken the impact procrastination has on your life. Along the way, you'll improve your productivity and become a healthier, happier, and more successful person.

A good way to illustrate the relationship between change and awareness is to consider a smoker who's trying to quit.

He needs to recognize that smoking is doing considerable harm to his health and make the conscious decision to quit. He needs to recognize the first sign of a craving and find a way to resist the temptation. He needs to see that if he gives in to the craving this time, he's more likely to smoke again next time. He needs to realize that he's most likely to smoke when he's drinking, and prepare his willpower beforehand.

The more awareness he has about his triggers for smoking, the better he'll fare.

Without awareness, he'd have no chance whatsoever. He'd be running on complete autopilot, following the monkey's impulses and urges without even realizing it. He'd fail at all of his attempts to quit and keep smoking for the rest of his life without ever having a clue of what went wrong.

It's the same with procrastination. We need to be aware of what's going on. Only then do we get the chance to change anything.

If you don't realize that the act of procrastination will always lead to more procrastination in the future, you will keep running into trouble. If you don't see that you'll never "feel more like it tomorrow," you'll always rationalize your decision to delay. If you don't recognize that distractions are a major reason for your procrastination, you won't get rid of them.

The more awareness you have about the details of your procrastination, the better equipped you'll be to change. I would go as far as saying that the more awareness you have, the less you'll procrastinate.

You see, awareness is oftentimes enough. Once we see what's going on, we almost automatically do the right things.

Now, here's the funny and challenging thing about awareness: We think we're good at it, but we're actually terrible at it.

Most of our choices are made on complete autopilot, without awareness of our underlying motivations or future consequences.

In fact, research shows we often don't realize we're making a choice in the first place. Consider a study which asked people how many decisions related to food they made in a day. What would you say? The average guess was 14.

In reality, when the same study participants were told to carefully track their decisions, the average they came up with was a whopping 227 food-related decisions every day!

That's more than 200 daily decisions people were unaware of — and those are just choices related to food.

How can you improve something when you're not even aware that there is something to improve upon?

When you're not aware of what's happening, your monkey is running the show and guiding your choices. You are just following your urges and impulses without even knowing it.

The point is this: If you want to overcome procrastination, you need to increase your awareness of its many aspects. You need to pay a little more attention. You need to become a curious scientist — constantly watching, studying, and tweaking your own behavior.

The good news is that you'll automatically increase your awareness simply by reading this book and learning more about the topic of procrastination. Once you know some of the science and theory behind it, you'll start detecting patterns in your life.

The mere act of detecting these patterns will help you facilitate change. (Yes, by merely reading this book, you'll get better at eliminating procrastination!)

More awareness is always a good thing, so I suggest using another strategy that will help raise awareness around your behavior and habits related to procrastination. It's called a *procrastination log*.

TRY THIS: Keep a Procrastination Log

One of the best ways to increase your awareness of procrastination is to keep a log in which you track avoided activities, excuses, rationalizations, emotions, specific thoughts, and so on.

This record of your current behavior helps you see recurring patterns, learn from mistakes, and prepare better next time.

I suggest using a simple three-row spreadsheet with the rows "avoided activity," "explanation," and "plan."

Here are some examples you may recognize from your own life (it's not displayed in table format here because Kindle wouldn't display it properly):

Avoided activity: Doing homework.
Explanation: I was doing homework when Mike called and asked me to come over and try his new video game. I said yes and never got around to finishing my homework.
Plan: Next time I'm working on my homework, I'll put my phone on airplane mode.

Avoided activity: Getting up early
Explanation: I wanted to get up at 6 a.m. today, but I hit the snooze button and slept until 9 a.m.
Plan: Read the following implementation intention (see chapter five for more on that) before going to bed: "As soon as the alarm clock goes off, I immediately get out of bed — no matter what!" If the problem persists, I'll create a commitment contract (see chapter six for more on that).

Avoided activity: Exercise

Explanation: I wanted to exercise after work today. Unfortunately I was a bit tired and told myself that it wasn't worth it if I don't have enough energy. That was, of course, just a lame excuse.
Plan: I can make exercising after work easier by preparing everything beforehand. From now on, I'll pack everything I need for exercising in the morning. I am also creating a plan: "When I get home from work, I immediately grab my training bag and head to the gym — no matter what."

Avoided activity: Studying for an exam
Explanation: I wanted to study on Sunday, but my friends urged me to go partying with them. I went, got completely hammered, woke up with a hangover, and couldn't get myself to study in that condition.
Plan: If my friends ask me to come party this weekend, I'll immediately answer in the following way, "Thanks, but no. I really need to study." Alternatively, I can still go partying but drink less. In that case, I can use the following implementation intention for myself: "After my first two beers, I will stop drinking for the rest of the night."

Avoided activity: Paying the bills
Explanation: For whatever reason, I just kept delaying paying the bills and now have to pay a fine.
Plan: From now on, I'll use the following plan: "Next time I get a bill, I immediately pay it."

These examples will hopefully give you a better understanding of awareness and why it's so important.

To make sure you can fully grasp the idea, I want to finish the chapter with a story from my own life. I believe the story beautifully illustrates just what a crucial part awareness can play in our lives.

A few weeks ago, a friend of mine visited for coffee. During our conversation, he realized he had forgotten to work out that day, saying something along the lines of, "Oh, shit. I wanted to work out today. I must have forgotten. Ah, well…"

That was a moment of awareness. He became aware of the fact that he had wanted to do one thing, but ended up doing something else. Great! That's the beginning of positive change.

Unfortunately for him, he simply shrugged it off and made no big deal out of it.

What a shame! If he had paid just a little more attention, allocated just a little time to self-reflection, he could have learned so much.

He could, for example, have realized that this happens to him all the time. He could have realized that this pattern plays out like clockwork in his life. He could have realized that he didn't exercise because he told himself that he'll feel more like doing it tomorrow. He could have realized that he's in the habit of procrastinating when it comes to working out. He could have realized that this is an issue he needs to address. He could have realized that he needs to create a plan to guarantee he exercises regularly.

He missed a golden opportunity to learn from his mistakes. (I told him afterwards, by the way.)

And unless he starts paying more attention to his habit, thought, and behavior patterns, he's unlikely to ever get a handle on this particular issue. He'll keep running into the same trouble many times over. He'll find his health and fitness deteriorating without ever understanding the underlying causes behind it. He'll probably end up blaming his genetics or outside circumstances instead of taking a closer look at his own behavior.

Please don't make the same mistake.

Please pay a little more attention to your daily thoughts, emotions, and behaviors. Watch. Observe. Dissect. Analyze. Prepare. Repeat.

It has to be on a basis of constant trial-and-error — because that's how we get better.

And I can tell you from my own life that if you're willing to allocate time and effort to awareness, the rewards will come quickly and in abundance.

Chapter Summary

The idea: Successful change always starts with awareness. If you're not aware of what's going wrong in your life, how are you going to fix it? The more awareness you develop regarding your procrastination tendencies, the faster you'll change for the better.

The tactics

Keep a Procrastination Log: Keep a log in which you keep track of avoided activities, explanations for what happened, and how you plan to overcome the issue next time. The record of your current behavior helps you see recurring patterns, learn from mistakes, and prepare for the future.

Chapter 3

The Paradox of Getting Started — Why the Problem Is the Cure

What do the tasks you procrastinate on tend to have in common?

They all make you feel uncomfortable, anxious, or overwhelmed, don't they?

Sometimes it's almost as if you're feeling actual pain when thinking about such tasks, right?

Well, that's because contemplating certain tasks *does* cause actual, physical pain. When researchers put people in fMRI machines and ask them to think about doing a dreaded task, the pain regions of the participants' brains light up, signaling that they're experiencing tangible pain.

I'm not kidding. When you're thinking about doing the taxes, you feel actual pain. When you're thinking about exercising after work, you feel actual pain. When you're thinking about writing your dissertation, you feel actual pain.

No wonder so many of us keep procrastinating! Nobody likes to feel pain (except for the occasional masochist, I suppose).

And what's our natural inclination when facing painful things?

We shy away from them.

Once burned, twice shy.

Of course we want to avoid and put off certain tasks — they literally hurt us.

While some people can think about difficult tasks with no problems, procrastinators think about certain tasks and immediately start feeling bad. It's like I said in chapter one — procrastinators tend to have deep emotional scars that lead to having negative associations with certain tasks. It's not our fault that we feel this procrastination-causing pain, but it's our responsibility to learn how to handle it and function in spite of it.

Keep this in mind next time some smart-ass tells you something along the lines of, "Just do it already. What's the big deal?" Well, it's not that simple. And everyone who's ever struggled with procrastination knows that it's impossible to "just do it." That's exactly our problem — for whatever reason, we can't just do it. But I digress...

Coming back to experiencing pain when contemplating certain tasks, it may very well be that you're unaware of this pain in your day-to-day life. That's because it tends to happen unconsciously.

As an example, you may make the conscious plan to study after school today. At night, when going to bed, you may realize that you didn't do it. Whoops, what happened? Your unconscious mind steered you away from the pain, that's what happened.

To bring back our little analogy, the monkey urged you to run away from what feels painful and toward what feels better. You may have watched some TV, had a nice dinner, and gone out for a beer with your buddies — activities that feel good. That's the monkey unconsciously and automatically guiding your behavior away from pain and toward pleasure.

It will, of course, take a fair amount of awareness on your part to see these patterns operating in your own life.

And now for the good news.

Research shows that there's an easy way to get rid of the pain associated with certain tasks: Just. Get. Started.

As soon as you start engaging in a task, the pain evaporates. Barbara Oakley, an expert on student procrastination, explains in her book *A Mind For Numbers*:

"We procrastinate about things that make us feel uncomfortable. Medical imaging studies have shown that mathphobes, for example, appear to avoid math because even just thinking about it seems to hurt. The pain centers of their brains light up when they contemplate working on math.

But there's something important to note. It was the anticipation that was painful. When the mathphobes actually did math, the pain disappeared."

Fascinating, right?

The pain is in the anticipation, not in the actual performance of a dreaded task.

If you want relief from negative emotions caused by dreaded tasks, you can either procrastinate, which simply postpones the pain, or you can just get started on the task (easier said than done, but strategies are coming). Once you get started, the pain evaporates.

And this near-instant pain relief isn't the only thing that's happening when we get started. Other research shows that the mere act of getting started powerfully shifts our perception of the task and ourselves. Timothy A. Pychyl, a leading procrastination researcher, explains in his book *Solving The Procrastination Puzzle*:

"Surprisingly, we found a change in the participants' perceptions of their tasks. On Monday, the dreaded, avoided task was perceived as very stressful, difficult, and unpleasant. On Thursday (or the wee hours of Friday morning), once they had actually engaged in the task they had avoided all week, their perceptions changed. The ratings of task stressfulness, difficulty, and unpleasantness decreased significantly… In fact, many participants made comments when we paged them during their last-minute efforts that they wished they had started earlier — the task was actually interesting, and they thought they could do a better job with a little more time."

Once you get started, you realize it's not nearly as bad as you thought.

The task isn't as daunting, unpleasant, difficult, or stressful as you've imagined. Heck, it's actually kind of fun and interesting. And hey! You're not as lazy and unproductive as you thought. You *can* do this! You *can* be disciplined and get things done!

Better yet, you're now actively working on your task and are probably making great progress. Making progress feels great and so your mood, optimism, and self-confidence get another nice little boost. All of a sudden, you're feeling upbeat, positive, optimistic, and confident in yourself — you now have some powerful positive momentum on your side.

The small act of getting started creates ripple effects and sets in motion a whole machinery of self-perpetuating upward spirals. As you get started, pain goes away, perceptions change, and you start creating momentum.

It's like Newton's law of inertia states: "An object at rest stays at rest and an object in motion stays in motion."

It's all about making that important switch from non-doing to doing.

That's what procrastination comes down to: moving from non-doing to doing. A large part of overcoming procrastination means getting better at making that switch.

The good news is that you become better and better at making the switch every single time you do it.

Every time you overcome the motivational surface tension and move from non-doing to doing, you get better at it. Every time you manage to get started on difficult tasks, you build up that muscle of bursting through resistance and doing what needs to get done whether you feel like it or not.

Everything counts here. You either reinforce the pattern of needless delay, or the pattern of getting started and overcoming resistance.

Now you may interject, "But Nils, this is exactly my problem! I just can't get started!"

You're right. Getting started is simultaneously the root of the problem and its solution. If you can't get yourself to begin a task, if you can't resist the pull of the monkey, you'll end up procrastinating. If you are able to get started, on the other hand, procrastination gets nipped in the bud.

To overcome procrastination, you need to get better at getting started, vetoing the monkey, overcoming resistance, handling negative emotions — call it whatever you want.

Ultimately, most of the tactics in this book will help you with that in one way or another.

For now, let's look at five specific short-term strategies that you can start using immediately.

TRY THIS: Focus On The Next Step, Not The Next Thousand Steps

A major reason many of us procrastinate is because we're overwhelmed.

It's an uncomfortable feeling that is sure to get our monkey out of its cage. The monkey wants to run away from the uncomfortable feelings and, as a result, we become resistant to the task and experience an urge to do something more enjoyable.

Because of that, we tend to be especially vulnerable to procrastination when facing big projects, which are naturally challenging and overwhelming. All those options, unknowns, and uncertainties are almost unbearable for the monkey, which is why it tends to run rampant when you're contemplating large projects. Where should you even start? What's the first priority? What's a reasonable deadline? What are all the things that still need to get done?

It's almost impossible to get started if all those overwhelming thoughts are swirling around your head.

The key to overcoming this type of procrastination is to simplify things by breaking the project down into small, actionable steps.

First, create a list of all the things you'll need to get done. Second, create a plan — which tasks are you tackling first and in which order? Third, stop worrying about the steps further down the list and start focusing only on the very next step. Fourth, just get started on that very next step.

Stop worrying about getting it all done. Stop worrying about all the things left to do. Stop worrying about what's still to come. Just keep focusing on the very next step.

Theodore Roosevelt once said: "I dream of men who take the next step instead of worrying about the next thousand steps."

And Mark Twain seemed to agree when he said, "The secret of getting ahead is getting started. The secret of getting started is breaking your complex overwhelming tasks into small manageable tasks, and then starting on the first one."

So, get in the habit of focusing on one thing only: the next actionable step. And then get started on that. Do not permit yourself to worry about the next thousand steps — that's a surefire way to get overwhelmed and procrastinate.

John Steinbeck, a Nobel Prize winning author, explains it perfectly: "When I face the desolate impossibility of writing 500 pages, a sick sense of failure falls on me and I know I can never do it. Then, gradually, I write one page and then another. One day's work is all I can permit myself to contemplate."

Don't allow yourself to look too far ahead. One small and actionable task is all you can allow yourself to contemplate.

Inch by inch, life's a cinch; yard by yard, life is hard.

Now, fair warning: This tactic isn't as easy as it may sound. It takes effort and willpower. You'll have to actively divert your focus from the overwhelming aspects of a project, then funnel it onto the next actionable step.

As long as you're able to keep your focus tight like that, your monkey will be humming along without disturbing you.

TRY THIS: Lower Your Ridiculous Standards

High standards are bad news for anyone prone to procrastinate.

What do I mean by having high standards? High standards are when you think you have to do things perfectly or they're not worth doing at all. It's when you think you have to meditate 20 minutes every morning as a beginning meditator. It's when you think you have to exercise four to five times a week when you're currently a couch potato. It's when you think you need the perfect business plan before being able to start a business. It's when I think my first Kindle book needs to be the best book on procrastination ever written (guilty as charged!).

High standards create a multitude of problems for procrastinators.

First of all, high standards make it hard to get started. Think about it — the higher your standard, the harder getting started becomes. As you're moving the hurdle higher, you're making it more difficult to climb over.

Put differently, your initial resistance to getting started grows as your standard grows. The higher your standard, the greater your resistance. Sitting down to meditate for one minute (low standard) is easy. Sitting down to meditate for 20 minutes (high standard) scares the crap out of most people. Which are you more likely to get started on?

In addition to that, high standards set us up for a cycle of failure, self-criticism, and procrastination. When you inevitably fail to meet your high standards, chances are you beat yourself up over it. You feel like a loser. You get demoralized, drown yourself in self-pity, and end up even more likely to procrastinate again in the future. (We'll talk more about self-criticism and its detrimental effects on procrastination in chapter 8.)

The solution is to lower your standards.

Make winning easy.

Aim to meditate for one minute a day, not 20 minutes. Aim to go for a walk a few times a week, not exercise daily. Aim to do five pushups, not a one-hour full body workout. Aim to work on writing your Kindle book for 20 minutes, not a couple of hours.

Keep in mind that you can always do more. Once you've overcome the initial resistance, you can meditate, exercise, or write for as long as you'd like. The key is to lower the bar for getting started. That allows you to get in motion without feeling intimidated. And once you're in motion, Newton's law of inertia states that you'll stay in motion.

The beauty of lowering your standards is that it allows you to just get started. And once you get started, good things start happening.

Don't let perfect be the enemy of the good is a good motto to follow.

TRY THIS: Follow the Two-Minute Rule

Invented by productivity expert David Allen, the two-minute rule states that if a task takes less than two minutes to complete, do it immediately.

Instead of answering simple yes or no emails "later," do so right after opening them. Instead of leaving the dishes in the sink for hours after cooking, wash them right after cooking or eating. Instead of bringing out the garbage "later," do it right when the garbage bin is full. Instead of needlessly delaying paying your bills, pay them right after getting them in the mail.

Stop filling your mind or to-do list with an endless array of small tasks. Instead, get in the habit of ticking them off right when they appear.

Not only will this reduce how overwhelmed you are, free up a lot of mental space, and give you a small sense of accomplishment, but it will also get you in the habit of starting and finishing. Before you know it, getting started on small tasks becomes second nature. And sooner or later, that habit translates into the habit of getting started on bigger tasks and projects too.

Just following this simple rule helps you rewire your brain to get started on tasks, get more things done, and procrastinate less. Easy, yet effective.

TRY THIS: Set an Implementation Intention

Implementation intentions are simple "if-then" plans designed to program your unconscious mind to act in a desired way in a specific future situation. For the "if" part, you pick a cue — e.g., a specific time, a thought, an emotion, or anything else — and for the "then" part, you pick a desired action.

"If situation X arises, then I will perform response Y."

If such and such happens, then I will do such and such. If I get home from work, then I'll cook a healthy dinner. If I feel the urge to procrastinate, then I'll just ignore it.

These plans sound simple and somewhat naïve, but they can be incredibly effective. They're sometimes referred to as "instant habits" because of their power to unconsciously guide our behavior in positive ways. We'll get more into the details in chapter five, which is solely focused on implementation intentions.

For now, let's form some implementation intentions designed to help you get started. Note that it's not necessary to use the specific if-then structure. As long as you link a cue with a behavior, you're good to go.

Here are a couple of ideas:

- When I get home from work today, then I will immediately pack my gym bag and head to the gym to do my workout.

- If I catch myself thinking "I'll feel more like it tomorrow," then I'll just get started on some aspect of the task.

- If I feel too tired to do something, then I'll just ignore it and get started anyway.

- Saturday morning after breakfast, I'll immediately start studying for my upcoming math exam.

- After watching 30 minutes of TV, I'll immediately get started on writing my dissertation.

TRY THIS: Focus on the Process, Not the Outcome

An outcome is always the result of a process.

If you follow the right process long enough, you will eventually achieve the outcome as a natural by-product.

If you eat healthy, sleep well, and exercise regularly, then you will lose weight. If you write 1,000 words every day, then you will finish your book. If you play football every day, then you will become more skilled at that sport. If you study for your exams for hours every day, then you will get good grades.

During your journey from where you are to where you want to go, you can either focus on the process or the outcome.

If you're trying to lose weight, you can either step on the scale every day and measure your weight, or you can forget about the scale and just focus on making sure that you eat healthy every day. Likewise, if you're trying to build more muscle mass, you can focus on your weight and what you look like in the mirror, or you can trust the process and focus on eating well and going to the gym regularly.

When you're trying to get started on an unappealing, difficult, or otherwise uncomfortable task, it's best if you forget about the outcome and just focus on the process.

It's usually the outcome that is associated with negative emotions, not the process. Writing a 500-page novel (the outcome) scares the crap out of anyone. Writing for 30 to 60 minutes every morning (the process) is a lot more appealing.

Next time you're trying to work on something you tend to procrastinate on, simply set a timer for 20 to 30 minutes. Tell yourself you're going to work on this thing for 20 to 30 minutes. That's it. It's that easy. It's nothing to be scared of.

Setting a timer helps you focus on the process and reduces a lot of the friction associated with getting started. You literally calm down your overactive brain and help it stop worrying about all the nonsense it tends to get caught up in. In other words, you stop scaring your monkey and soothe it instead (the negative emotions associated with the outcome tend to get it all amped up).

You simplify things. You make it easy. And before you know it, you've started and good things ensue.

Chapter Summary

The main idea: Learning ways to get started on tasks is a massive step toward overcoming procrastination. By definition, if you can't get yourself to begin a task, you procrastinate. If you manage to get started, you stop procrastination dead in its tracks. You also realize that the task isn't as bad as you thought, start feeling better about yourself, and create powerful momentum because you're making progress.

The tactics

Focus on the next step, not the next thousand steps. Use your willpower to move your attention away from the overwhelming aspects of a project and narrow it down to the next actionable task you can get started on.

Lower your perfectionistic standards. Decrease your initial resistance to getting started by lowering your standards. For example, aim to meditate for one minute, not 20 minutes.

Follow the two-minute rule. If a task takes less than two minutes to complete, do it immediately.

Set an implementation intention. Use the formula, "If situation X arises, then I will perform response Y." A common example: "If I get home after work, then I'll immediately start studying for my upcoming math exam."

Focus on the process, not the outcome. Set a timer for 20 to 30 minutes and focus on the process of working on a dreaded task for that predetermined amount of time.

Chapter 4

What Productivity Gurus Won't Tell You About Procrastination — Why Time Management Is Only Part of the Solution

Some people will tell you that procrastination is primarily a time management issue.

Don't listen to these people. They have no idea what they're talking about. Procrastination, at its very core, is an emotion management problem, not a time management problem.

Let me give you an example to illustrate why that's true. There were times in the past where I would plan out my days perfectly from a time management perspective. I had my morning ritual, then some work, then a short walk, then some more work, then lunch, and so on. I had it all planned out in detail. Any time management guru would have been proud of me.

Here's what happened despite all of that: More often than not, I just couldn't get myself to do what I had so beautifully planned. I *wanted* to follow through with my morning ritual. I *wanted* to follow through with tackling the most challenging task of the day first (eat that frog, right?). I *wanted* to follow through with going on a walk after the first work period. I just couldn't get myself to do it. The resistance — the negative emotions associated with certain tasks — was just too much to handle and I procrastinated.

It wasn't a time management issue, it was an emotion management issue. I procrastinated because I couldn't deal with the negative emotions, not because I was suffering from bad time management.

If you let your monkey run the show, time management will not be enough. You can have the best time management skills in the world and still suffer from a crazy and crippling amount of procrastination.

With that being said, good time management can, of course, be very helpful.

So while time management isn't a complete solution (and not the primary focus of this guide), it's still a necessary part of the solution.

In this chapter, we'll discuss three basic time management strategies. If you get these down, you'll benefit greatly from improved clarity and productivity. You'll procrastinate less, and you'll be well-positioned to use the other procrastination tactics because you're now operating from a solid time management foundation.

Onwards!

TRY THIS: Schedule, Schedule, Schedule

Here's the first rule of time management: "What gets scheduled gets done. What doesn't get scheduled doesn't get done."

You probably have a to-do list, either on paper or in your head, with the things you'd like to get done today, tomorrow, or sometime in the more distant future. And while having a list is great, it's only the first step. The real magic happens when you start scheduling exactly *when* you're going to do the things on your list.

You see, unless you take what's on your list and put it on the calendar, it's not real. It's just an idea on a piece of paper. Something that might get done.

But the moment you schedule it, it becomes real (which is probably why we're so resistant to the idea of scheduling in the first place).

One thing I tend to procrastinate on is going to the hairdresser. For days and weeks, I know I should go and have the idea swirling around in my head. Sometimes I even write it down on my to-do list.

But until I schedule an exact time and date, you can be sure that I keep further delaying it, "Today I have so much energy. I shouldn't waste it." "The weather is too beautiful. I should do something outside." "It's not that bad yet. I can wait another week."

Once you schedule something, you immediately short circuit all the rationalizations and excuses holding you back.

A few years ago, I came across a great study illustrating the powers of scheduling things. 20 drug addicts were asked to write a résumé before five p.m. that day. They were encouraged to do so because it might help them find work after leaving rehab. One group of addicts was told to clearly define when and where they would write the résumé. The other half were merely told to write their résumé at a time and place of their choosing.

One group had to schedule it and the other didn't. The results? At five p.m., eight of the 10 addicts who clearly defined when and where they would write the résumé had actually written it. Of the 10 addicts who didn't schedule, none (!) of them had written it.

It's a simple, but powerful truth worth remembering: *What gets scheduled gets done. What doesn't get scheduled doesn't get done.*

If you want to procrastinate less, get in the habit of using a calendar and transferring items on your lists onto that calendar.

TRY THIS: Start Your Day On Fire

Has the following scenario ever happened to you?

Your alarm clock wakes you up way too early in the morning. You're still dead tired and you hit the snooze button a bunch of times. When you finally manage to crawl out of bed, you already feel like a loser because you got up late.

You rush through your morning ritual, but skip certain parts because you simply don't have the time. You then rush to work and eat a bagel on your way there. You arrive late, feeling exhausted, tired, and stressed out.

You have no idea what your most important tasks are, don't feel like finding out, and decide to check your email, Facebook, and read some news instead. Before you know it, 30 minutes have passed and you haven't gotten anything done yet. You start feeling guilty. Worst of all, you still don't feel like working on important projects.

What the hell just happened? The day has barely even started and you're already bathing in a soup of guilt, stress, disappointment, and other negative emotions.

Now remember why we procrastinate: to run away from negative emotions. Guess what happens when you start your day like that? Exactly. You'll want to run away from those painful feelings. You'll distract yourself, you'll feel even guiltier, and you'll basically procrastinate all day long.

Once you're in that procrastination-laziness-distraction-negativity mode, it's hard to get out again. This is Newton's law of inertia all over again: an object in motion stays in motion; an object at rest stays at rest.

Once you're dillydallying, you tend to keep doing it all day long. And because you're feeling guilty, disappointed, and ashamed for not being productive, actually doing something worthwhile becomes almost impossible. Basically, your monkey is now running the show.

You see, the first few hours of the day are of incredible importance. If you mess them up, chances are you're screwed for the entire day. You've got so much negative momentum going on that it's highly unlikely you'll be able to turn things around.

Thankfully, this works both ways. If you dominate the first few hours of the day, you're well on your way to a highly productive day with very little procrastination. Once you're being productive and disciplined, you tend to stay productive and disciplined. You're building positive momentum. You're getting things done, are making progress, and feel good about yourself, maybe even a little proud. All those positive emotions fuel your motivation and keep you buzzing all day long.

I can't stress this enough: If you want to procrastinate less, you need to begin your day on fire. You need to get out of bed immediately after waking up. You need to patiently complete your morning ritual, eat a healthy breakfast, and start working on important and meaningful tasks at work. No goofing off. No warming up. No procrastinating early in the day.

And now, the million-dollar question: How can you make sure you don't mess up those crucial first few hours of the day? It's actually quite simple. You need to plan your day the night before. You need to know exactly what you're going to do in those first few hours. You need a clear step-by-step script that you can follow without having to think. This is what the last time management tip is all about.

TRY THIS: Plan Your Day the Night Before

Planning your day the night before is crucial for a number of reasons.

First of all, knowing exactly what you're going to do in the morning allows you to hit the ground running. This gives you the opportunity to make progress, feel good about yourself, and generate that all-important positive momentum.

Planning your day the night before is almost a guarantee that you'll get into action mode early in the day. And once you're in that action mode — being productive and disciplined — you tend to stay in it all day long.

Planning also helps eliminate any moments of, "Hmm, what should I do now?" It's during these moments that we're most vulnerable to procrastination. Instead of figuring out the most important tasks (which is uncomfortable, and therefore brings out the monkey), we tend to do what's convenient and urgent. Or even worse, we just waste our time on Facebook.

With that being said, let's briefly talk about how to plan your day. To begin with, create a list of all the activities you must and want to incorporate into the following day. This list includes fixed appointments (like work, doctor's appointments, or meetings) and high-value activities (like important projects, meditation, exercise, or reading).

Once you have your list of activities, simply drag and drop them into your calendar. First, add the fixed appointments. Then add your high-value activities around the fixed appointments.

Personally, I tend to only plan my mornings in detail, while leaving the rest of the day open and flexible. Today's plan looked like this:

1. Exercise

2. Cold shower

3. Meditate

4. Write some of this book

5. Take a walk outside as a break

6. Keep writing on this book.

That's it. That was my entire plan. It took me 30 seconds to create and ensured that I started my day on fire while building that all-important positive momentum.

Chapter Summary

The idea: While time management isn't a complete solution to procrastination, it's still a very helpful tool and a necessary foundation to build upon.

The tactics

Schedule, schedule, schedule. What gets scheduled gets done. Get in the habit of moving tasks from your to-do list to your calendar. When exactly are you going to get something done? (If you don't currently use a calendar, I highly suggest starting now.)

Start your day on fire. Be as disciplined and productive in the early morning as you possibly can be. No time-wasting. No dillydallying. No goofing off. Follow your plan — whether you feel like it or not! Create that all-important momentum and remember: Once you're in action mode, you'll tend to stay in it all day long.

Plan your day the night before. Get in the habit of creating a step-by-step outline for the next day (at least for the first few hours). You should be able to go through the early morning hours without having to think much.

Chapter 5

The Magic of a Simple Plan — How to Program Your Unconscious Mind to Automatically Procrastinate Less

Wouldn't it be great if you could program yourself to act in any way you like in the future?

If you could just write a code for behavior and then automatically find yourself following that code?

If you could plan today how you would act tomorrow?

Well, good news — you can do exactly that with the use of implementation intentions, which we've briefly discussed in chapter two. As you may recall, implementation intentions are if-then plans that predetermine how you will act in a specific future situation. They look like this:

"If _____ happens, then I will do _____."

You are linking a cue (the "if" part) with a desired behavior (the "then" part).

"As soon as I wake up, I'll immediately get out of bed." "If I'm done eating, then I'll immediately wash all the dishes and clean the kitchen."

You decide *now* how you're going to act in the *future*.

This allows you to make decisions from a place of calm and rationality. You get to ask yourself, "What would be the best way to act if such and such happens? What would I like to do if such and such happened? What would I like to do after finishing XYZ?"

Implementation intentions may sound too simplistic to be effective, but they're actually one of modern psychology's most studied and proven methods to positively change people's behavior.

In the remainder of this chapter, we'll discuss why implementation intentions work and look at some of the scientific proof of their effectiveness. At the end, you'll create your personal implementation intentions with the help of my examples.

Why Do Implementation Intentions Work So Well?

It's fascinating what happens in our brains when we're forming these implementation intentions.

First, a link is being created between the cue and the desired behavior.

If you wanted to go to the gym after coming home from work, you'd create the following plan: "As soon as I come home from work, I'll head to the gym." In this case, the cue "coming home from work" would be linked with the behavior "heading to the gym".

Next, the cue becomes heavily activated in your brain. This means that the cue is just dying to get noticed. It's kind of like the school kid raising its hand in excitement and trying to get the teacher's attention.

Without any conscious effort or awareness of your own, your brain is now constantly scanning the environment in search of that cue (e.g., "coming home from work").

Once your brain detects the cue, the real magic starts happening.

Because cue and behavior have already been linked, your brain automatically executes your predetermined plan. You'll find yourself packing your stuff and heading to the gym whether you're aware of it or not. Your unconscious mind simply takes over and executes your plan on your behalf.

Sometimes you realize what's happening and sometimes you don't. Either way, you'll find yourself doing the right thing.

That's really the beauty and elegance of this intervention: that most of it happens below your level of conscious awareness. You can be busy doing other things while your brain is scanning the environment for you, detecting cues and guiding behavior. Some people refer to implementation intentions as "instant habits" because of their automatic and unconscious nature.

And just like real habits, implementation intentions not only unconsciously and automatically guide your behavior; they also impact your willpower in desirable ways.

For starters, they conserve your willpower because you're not required to make conscious decisions when their habitual nature takes over. Preserving willpower means there will be more left in the tank to veto the monkey — to fight temptations and get done what needs to get done.

In addition to that, you're also able to better overcome bouts of low willpower. When you automatically do the right thing, it doesn't matter if your willpower is depleted or not. (If you're confused about the willpower thing, don't get hung up. We'll discuss it in detail in chapter 10.)

So that's why implementation intentions work in theory. Now let's see the proof...

The Proof Is in the Pudding

Believe it or not, implementation intentions have been proven effective in changing people's behavior in over 100 studies.

They've been shown to help people lose weight, quit smoking, eat healthier, drive more carefully, and more.

One study asked students before Christmas break if they wanted to participate in an experiment of how people spend their holidays.

Students who agreed were instructed to write an essay describing how they spent their Christmas, which had to be mailed in within two days of Christmas Eve. Half of the participants were given another instruction: to decide when and where they were going to write their essay. In other words, they were told to create an implementation intention.

The results speak for themselves. Two days after Christmas, 71% of students who predetermined when and where to write the essay had sent it in, compared to just 32% of students who didn't create implementation intentions. Think about that. Taking 30 seconds to create a simple if-then plan more than *doubled* the success rates of students.

Another study looked at tenth graders on summer break. They all had the goal of studying for their upcoming PSAT test in fall. In May, the researchers gave students a book with 10 PSAT practice tests and told them they would collect the book again in September when they returned to school. One group of students was also asked to decide when and where they would work on the practice problems over the summer months (e.g., "Monday through Thursday after breakfast in my room"). The students did not get a single reminder from the researchers over the summer.

After collecting the books from the students in September, the differences between the planners and non-planners was drastic. While non-planners completed an average of 100 problems, planners completed a staggering 250 problems. Again, performance more than doubled — all from one intention that took less than a few minutes to create.

Another experiment was designed to help people quit smoking through the use of implementation intentions. The results? Planners smoked significantly fewer cigarettes than non-planners over a period of two months. More importantly, 12% of planners quit smoking completely, as compared to only 2% of non-planners.

It doesn't matter what you're trying to accomplish; implementation intentions will increase your chances of succeeding significantly.

Heidi Grant Halvorson, an expert on the science of goal achievement, sums up the benefits of implementation intentions perfectly in her book *Succeed*:

"Gollwitzer and his colleague Paschal Sheeran recently reviewed the results from ninety-four studies that measured the effects of if-then planning and found significantly higher rates of goal attainment for just about every goal you can think of: using public transportation more frequently, buying organic foods, helping others, driving more carefully, not drinking, not starting smoking, remembering to recycle, following through on New Year's resolutions, negotiating fairly, avoiding stereotypical and prejudicial thoughts, doing math problems... you name the goal, and these simple plan will help you reach it."

She adds:

"Planning when, where, and how you will take the actions needed to reach your goal is probably the single most effective thing you can do to increase your chances of success."

Implementation intentions are an incredibly powerful and flexible tool to add to your arsenal.

Let's look at some practical applications for helping you win the procrastination battle.

TRY THIS: Set Some Implementation Intentions

Take a few minutes to think about your own procrastination habits.

What tasks do you tend to procrastinate on? When are you most prone to procrastinate? What activities would you like to engage in more often? What new habits would you like to build?

As you're thinking about procrastination in your own life, you'll realize there are lots of possibilities for using implementation intentions.

Write down some if-then plans for your best ideas and repeat them out loud or in your head a couple of times.

And don't worry about keeping your plans in the specific if-then formula. As long as you're linking a cue with a desired behavior, you're ready to rock it.

Below are some specific examples you can copy, modify, or use as inspiration. They are designed to help you overcome many procrastination-related problems such as not getting started, resisting temptations, overcoming times of low willpower, and so on.

- If I feel overwhelmed by a large project, then I can break it down into small, actionable steps and get started on step one.

- If I get bored during studying, then I'll ignore it and just keep going.

- If I get discouraged during writing, then I'll ignore it and just keep going.

- If I feel like hitting the snooze button, then I'll immediately get out of bed.

- If I feel like delaying an important task, then I'll immediately get started on a small aspect of the task.

- Saturday after breakfast, I'll start studying for my upcoming exam.

- If I find myself making excuses such as "I'm too tired" or "I'll feel more like it tomorrow" or "I work better under pressure," then I'll just ignore them and get started on a small aspect of the task.

- If I feel like watching TV, then I'll ignore it and keep working.

- As soon as I get home after work, I'll immediately prepare a healthy dinner.

- When it's time to go to bed, I'll write in my gratitude journal for five minutes.

Chapter Summary

The idea: Implementation intentions are a great strategy for tweaking your own behavior. These simple if-then plans literally program your unconscious mind and guide you to automatically act in desirable, procrastination-disabling ways.

The tactics

Create implementation intentions: Look at your own life and you will find endless opportunities to use if-then plans. Once you have something in mind, use the following formula to program your behavior: *"If _____ happens, then I will do _____."*

Chapter 6

Carrots & Sticks — They May Be Old School… But They Work!

In this chapter, we'll look at the motivational powers of carrots (rewards) and sticks (punishments).

Carrots and sticks work by influencing the monkey in your brain.

As you may recall from chapter one, the monkey refers to the part of your brain that operates on a very basic guiding principle: Approach what feels good (the carrot) and avoid what feels bad (the stick).

This part of our brain is stronger in some people and weaker in others. Put differently, some people are blessed with a relatively quiet monkey, while others are cursed with a monkey that's totally out of control and basically running the show 24/7. As procrastinators, we tend to have an out of control monkey. (We'll talk about long-term strategies to tame the monkey and lower its impact on us in chapter 10.)

The problem with the monkey is that it doesn't care about the future at all. It only cares about what feels good right this very moment.

The rational part of the brain would like to exercise regularly in order to live longer, be healthier, and have more energy in the *future*. The rational part would like to meditate daily in order to reap huge emotional benefits in the *future*. The rational part would like to finish tasks on time, be productive, and lay the groundwork for a successful *future*.

The monkey, on the other hand, couldn't care less about what's good for the future. It doesn't understand future benefits; it's only interested in immediate gratification.

So whenever you suggest doing something that's slightly uncomfortable or difficult, but beneficial for the future, the monkey will revolt. It will urge you to run away from what feels bad *right now* and toward something that feels better *right now*.

That, in a nutshell, is why we procrastinate.

Now, here's the good news: Because we know the monkey's basic operating principles, we can influence it by using rewards (carrots) and punishments (sticks).

The goal is to add immediate rewards for positive activities and immediate punishments for negative activities. (The more immediate, the better.)

Instead of waiting for the benefits of meditation, exercise, or work, we can make them gratifying in the short-term. Instead of waiting for the negative effects of procrastinating, we can make ourselves pay for procrastination immediately.

In the remainder of this chapter, we'll discuss three specific ideas to put this knowledge into practice.

TRY THIS: Promise Yourself a Reward

If you promise yourself a million dollars for finishing your work project by Friday, chances are you'll get it done by Friday, if not earlier.

Lucky for us, smaller rewards do the trick as well.

As an example, you can promise yourself a delicious protein smoothie after exercising. You can promise yourself you'll go on a $200 shopping spree after finishing a work project. Or you can promise yourself you'll watch some TV after doing your homework.

The key to effective rewards is to make them as immediate as possible. It's best if they happen right after the desired behavior, such as a protein shake and a cookie after exercising, watching an episode of *Game of Thrones* after meditating, or dillydallying on Facebook after studying.

If you have a long project you're working on, it's best to promise yourself multiple small rewards for completing milestones *and* one bigger reward for completing the entire project.

By associating aversive tasks with rewards, you infuse them with some positive emotions, making them less appalling and more attractive for the monkey. This means less resistance, and ultimately less procrastination for you.

TRY THIS: Bundle Temptations

While the previous strategy is all about rewarding yourself *after* doing something, temptation bundling is all about rewarding yourself *while* you're doing it.

Temptation bundling means combining a temptation (something that feels good) with something you tend to procrastinate on. You're bundling a behavior you should do with a behavior you feel tempted to do.

This adds immediate gratification to aversive tasks, basically allowing the monkey to be a lot less reluctant about them.

Katy Milkman, the inventor of this strategy, came up with this idea due to her own needs. Here she talks about her struggles with procrastination and how temptation bundling helped her get a handle on it:

"What I realized is that if I only allowed myself to watch my favorite TV shows while exercising at the gym, then I'd stop wasting time at home on useless television, and I'd start craving trips to the gym at the end of a long day because I'd want to find out what happens next in my show. And not only that, I'd actually enjoy my workout and my show more combined. I wouldn't feel guilty watching TV, and time would fly while I was at the gym. So when I talk about temptation bundling, I mean combining a temptation — something like a TV show, a guilty pleasure, something that will pull you into engaging in a behavior — with something you know you should do but might struggle to do."

If you want to procrastinate less, choose a task you tend to delay and bundle it with one of your guilty pleasures.

Some common ideas are to watch TV while you're eating a healthy meal, listen to audiobooks while you're exercising, watch your favorite TV show while ironing or doing other household chores, or drink a cappuccino while working.

If you want, you can go a step further and *only* indulge in the temptations when also engaging in the positive behaviors. That would look as follows. *Only* watch TV while eating a healthy meal. *Only* listen to audiobooks while exercising. *Only* watch your favorite TV show while ironing or doing other household chores. *Only* drink cappuccinos while working.

And of course, you can use temptations for multiple good behaviors — e.g., only watch TV when you're eating something healthy, when you're ironing, when you're stretching, or when you're doing other household chores.

The basic idea is to make a dreaded task a bit more enticing. When I don't feel like working, for example, I'll sometimes "allow" myself to have another cup of coffee, some dark chocolate, or another treat. This is often enough for me to break through the initial resistance and just get started.

I'm also a regular user of smart drugs and will basically tell myself, "Okay, I'm going to try this new performance enhancer. In return, I'll work for another hour or two on this project."

You're basically negotiating with yourself. And it works.

TRY THIS: Make Procrastination Pay

Instead of rewarding yourself for getting something done (carrot), this strategy is all about punishing yourself for not getting something done (stick).

This approach tends to work better because of a concept called *loss aversion* — people's tendency to prefer avoiding losses to acquiring equivalent gains. It's better to not lose $10 than to find $10. Some research suggests that losses are twice as powerful as gains.

Here's how this tactic works: You give your buddy $100. If you complete your desired activity by, say, 9 p.m., you get your $100 back. If you don't, you lose the $100.

This is often referred to as a *commitment contract*. You commit to doing something (complete activity by 9 p.m.) and set a penalty for failing to keep your commitment (lose $100).

The penalty can be anything that creates massive pain for you — huge sums of money, doing something embarrassing in public, shaving your head, not going to your favorite festival, and so on.

The greater the pain you'll have to endure for failing, the better it'll work.

If you use money, make sure you put up the money beforehand. Don't say, "I'll give it to you when I fail." No, no, no. You give the money beforehand. If you want it back, get the thing done on time!

You can create such agreements with your mother, a trusted friend, or a third-party website such as stickk.com. Whatever option you choose, make sure that your referee actually pulls the trigger and executes the penalty. (Your mother may not be the best option.)

As is the case with rewards, it's best if you make the punishments as immediate as possible. If you've got a long-term project, don't just set one large punishment in case of missing the deadline. Set up punishments for missing milestones as well.

I'm currently using a commitment contract for finishing this book. I've handed over $150 to my brother Jonas and will only get it back when I finish the first draft before Friday (it's now Tuesday).

Update: It didn't work well at all. "Finishing the first draft" wasn't specific enough — there was no way for Jonas to determine whether I'd upheld my commitment or not. And because I knew that, I never felt any pressure to work harder than usual. Lesson learned: Make sure your commitment is highly specific. Your referee should know without a doubt whether you've upheld your end of the bargain.

Chapter Summary

The idea: The monkey in your brain operates on the simple principle of approaching what feels good (the carrot) and avoiding what feels bad (the stick). We can use this knowledge to our advantage by making desirable activities more attractive while making distractions and time-wasters less attractive. The result? Less procrastination.

The tactics

Promise Yourself a Reward: Attaching rewards to aversive tasks makes them more attractive for the monkey. In turn, you'll experience less resistance toward the task. As an example, you can reward yourself with a delicious protein smoothie after a hard workout session.

Temptation Bundling: Adding an enticing temptation to an aversive task allows you to make the task more appealing to the monkey. As a result, you'll feel less resistant toward the task. A common example is to exercise while listening to your favorite podcast.

Make Procrastination Pay: You can use so-called commitment contracts to associate massive pain with procrastinating on a specific task. This will increase your motivation and can all but guarantee you'll get the dreaded task done. An example could be giving your friend $500 and only getting it back if you show up at his door to exercise on time. If you don't show up (you procrastinate), you lose the money.

Chapter 7

Why Your Granny Doesn't Procrastinate — The Alarming Link Between Technology, Distractions, and Procrastination

Robin Sharma, a leadership coach and bestselling author, sums up modern world perfectly:

"We live in The Age of Dramatic Distraction. Many shiny toys to chase every waking moment yet so few of those pursuits create real value and grow a life brilliantly lived.

Too many of us are overscheduled, overconnected and overstimulated by all the noise, interruptions and complexity of current society. The cost of this way of operating? You'll arrive at the last hour of your final day and realize you spent your highest potential on your lowest leverage activities."

The average American worker on an average day spends 2.1 hours in distraction, is interrupted every 11 minutes, watches 4.7 hours of TV, checks email every six minutes, and spends a total of 1.72 hours on email.

In the 1970s, 4-5% of people indicated that they considered themselves as procrastinators; today that number is at 20-25% — a five-fold increase over the span of a few decades.

What caused that epic rise in procrastination?

You guessed it — modern-day distractions such as Facebook, email, smartphones, video games, TV shows, and so on.

Piers Steel, a procrastination researcher and author of *The Procrastination Equation*, says this about the relationship between distractions and procrastination:

"…proximity to temptation is one of the deadliest determinants of procrastination. [And] the more enticing the distraction, the less work we do."

The relationship between distractions and procrastination can be illustrated with the following graph (taken from *The Procrastination Equation*).

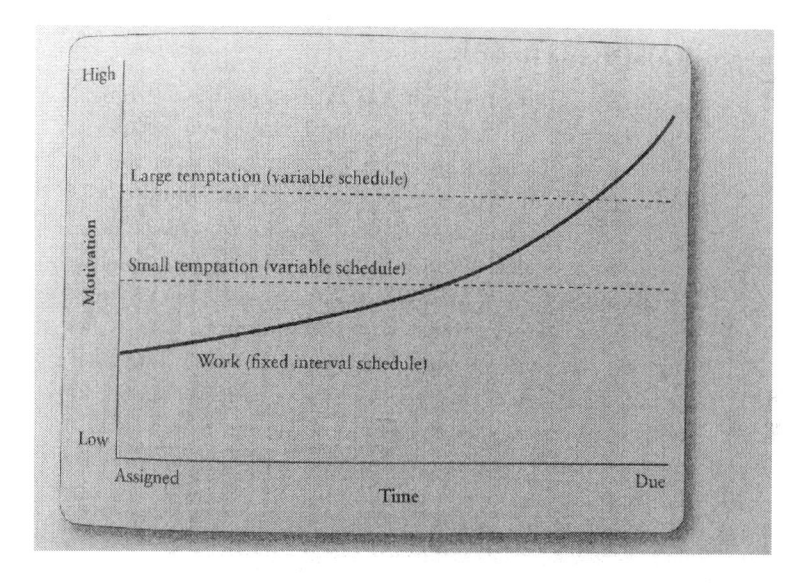

The solid line represents the work curve, which swoops up as the due date comes closer and closer. This shows that we tend to become increasingly more motivated the closer the deadline comes.

The dashed horizontal lines represent temptations. The higher the dashed lines go, the more enticing the temptations are and the more motivated we become to pursue them.

In this model, we procrastinate for as long as our work motivation is lower than our temptation motivation. Once the deadline is close enough, we become more motivated to work than to pursue a temptation — we stop procrastinating and start working.

As the graph shows, more enticing temptations lead to more procrastination.

In this way, the model beautifully illustrates how our modern world sets us up for failure.

Modern life creates more and more temptations, while at the same time making them more and more attractive. Put another way, modern life creates more and more dashed lines while also moving them higher and higher. The solid bar, on the other hand, hasn't seen any changes over the last decades. The pleasure derived from work is still the same as in the recent past.

To sum up: Temptations become more attractive while work starts looking increasingly boring and dull compared to them. The result? Procrastination.

If we look at this relationship, it becomes obvious why we've seen such an epic rise in procrastination since the 1970s.

Of course people in the 1970s didn't procrastinate as much... What were they going to do with their time, anyway? There was no internet, no smartphones, no video games, no Gameboys, no iPod, no iPad, no Facebook, no Instagram, no Snapchat...

Today, the internet alone is a candy land for procrastinators. In fact, it's now estimated that over 50% of time spent online is time spent procrastinating.

The only technology-driven distraction people in the 1970s had was a TV.

And even then, it's not comparable to today. TVs in the 1970s didn't have 500 channels. They didn't have high definition. They didn't have the ability to record everything. They didn't have the ability to buy movies or TV series. They didn't have any features to skip forwards or backwards.

My dad once told me that when he was a kid, the only program running on TV after 10 p.m. was "ants racing." There was simply no signal, and the only thing you saw when switching on the TV was a mixture of black and white dots, which, to my father, looked like ants racing.

It's abundantly clear that modern-day, technology-driven distractions are a major enabler of procrastination.

It's hard to meditate, exercise, read, or study when you could be watching TV, playing video games, or surfing the web. What do you think is more attractive to the monkey?

Oh, and the problem will only get worse.

The entertainment industry isn't exactly resting on their laurels. They keep refining their video games, online experiences, and TV features to make them more and more attractive and more and more addictive. And they're doing a great job at it — at the cost of your productivity and well-being!

If you want to even have a chance of overcoming procrastination and getting serious work done, you need to learn how to handle the allure of distractions.

In the remainder of this chapter, we'll look at three specific ways to do exactly that.

TRY THIS: Eliminate or Complicate

How often would you check Instagram if you could only access it on the roof of your house? Less often.

But you don't need to go to your roof to access Instagram, Facebook, video games, TVs, etc., do you?

The problem is most distractions are way too accessible. They're literally available to us in an instant.

Remember what we said earlier: Proximity to temptation is one of the deadliest determinants of procrastination. If we want to procrastinate less, we need to make distractions less readily accessible. We need to either completely eliminate a distraction, or complicate its access.

The good news is that's not hard to do at all. Here are some suggestions.

Block distracting websites. I'm talking about Facebook, Instagram, Snapchat, 9GAG, Gmail, news sites, and so on. You can block them on your laptop or computer using tools such as Cold Turkey. This tool allows you to schedule which websites you want to block and when. I personally find it very helpful. You can also block certain websites on your smartphone (I use an app called Trend Micro™ Mobile Security).

Delete distracting apps on your smartphone. I used to spend hours every day playing games, checking Facebook, or watching YouTube videos on my phone. Nowadays, distracting apps aren't even on my phone anymore — I just deleted them. It's radical, but it works.

Delete your computer games. During my high school years, I was addicted to an online game called Demigod. I spent well over 100,000 minutes playing that game, and I can tell you one thing: I never procrastinated more in my life than during those years. If you're serious about overcoming your procrastination issues, any online or computer game has to go. (At least temporarily. Consider it a form of rehab with the possibility of re-introducing some games back into your life at a later point in time.)

Sell your Nintendo Wii, Xbox, PlayStation, etc. And if that's too much, at least put them somewhere you don't see them. (As you're about to learn in the next tactic, "out of sight, out of mind" is a good motto.)

While these strategies aren't bulletproof, they will at least make it a lot harder for you to give in to temptations. Instead of opening your browser, typing "Fa," and entering Facebook, you now have to go into your website-disabling tool and somehow find a way to enable Facebook again.

The harder you make distractions to access, the less you'll procrastinate.

TRY THIS: Mold Your Environment

You've probably heard of *priming* before.

It states that everything in our environment unconsciously triggers an action or behavior in us.

Sexy images can trigger the urge to have sex. The smell of cake can trigger feelings of hunger. Putting sweets on someone's desk in a clear, rather than opaque bowl increases snacking. Watching people being friendly can make us kinder and more altruistic.

Certain things in your environment can trigger the urge to procrastinate, while other things can trigger you to work on your goals and stop putting things off.

To procrastinate less, we need to mold our environment so that it triggers us to work more. Anything that could trigger our urge to procrastinate needs to go. Anything that could trigger the action of working is welcome and can stay.

Here are some ideas on how to incorporate this into your life.

Declutter your browser. Every visible hotlink or bookmark can trigger unwanted goals that distract you from doing what needs to get done. Your browser should be as empty as possible. No bookmark bar. No other visible bookmarks. No visible hotlinks. No website suggestions when you open a new tab (I use the "Empty New Tab Page" Chrome extension). Your browser should not have any visible triggers at all.

Declutter your desktop. Same story. Quick launch icons and shortcuts can unconsciously trigger you to activate goals that are neither urgent nor important. Your desktop should be as clean and simplistic as possible. For instance, my desktop is a nature wallpaper with one folder that I've creatively titled "Desktop."

Put that phone away. Turn it off completely, or at least put it in airplane mode (remember, the harder you make distractions to access, the less you'll procrastinate). And please put your phone out of sight somehow. If you see it from where you are working, you'll always be unconsciously primed to have a quick glance. No, it won't be "just a minute!"

Eliminate all notifications. Every notification on your phone, laptop, or computer can distract you and trigger the urge to procrastinate. Go into your settings and eliminate *all* notifications.

Declutter your work and living space. A disorganized, cluttered, and messy space is like a minefield of potential distractions and unconscious goal triggers. If you want to get work done, you can't have your Xbox, smartphone, gym bag, books, and magazines all screaming for your attention. To procrastinate less, radically declutter your work and living space. Remove those triggers — out of sight, out of mind is the maxim.

Fill your environment with work triggers. What do you associate with your goals? What motivates you to get work done? What could unconsciously activate your goals? If you want to read a book at night, put it on your nightstand. If you want to write on a work project, put relevant material on your desk. If you want to feel more calm and mindful, put a small Buddha statue on your desk. If you want to feel inspired and motivated, fill your environment with images of some of your heroes. There are endless possibilities, and you can use anything as a trigger — quotes, Post-It notes, images, and so on.

You can either create an environment that supports your goals, or one that entices you to procrastinate. Your choice.

TRY THIS: Make Distractions Pay

Just like you can use commitment contracts to get your work done on time (see previous chapter), you can use them to make distractions less appealing.

If you must pay $500 every time you play a video game, you'll stop playing it immediately.

If you're serious about overcoming procrastination, this strategy can do wonders. Think about your worst temptations and create commitment contracts for them.

Let's take Facebook, for example. You could say that you allow yourself 15 minutes every day to spend on Facebook. Every additional minute costs you $10.

To set up a contract like that, you could do the following:

1) Download a tool called Rescue Time, which shows you your browsing activity.

2) Give a friend of yours, your mother, or someone else you trust $100 or any other amount of money.

3) Tell your trusted partner that you'll only get your money back if you send them a screenshot of Rescue Time at the end of the week.

4) Tell them to keep $10 for every additional minute you spent on Facebook.

It's by no means a perfect system, but it'll do the trick.

You can also use other third-party websites and tools to make this process easier. You can use Covenant Eyes (lets selected people see your website activities), stickk.com (the best website to create simple commitment contracts), SnuzNluz (makes you pay a certain amount of money every time you hit the snooze button), or Rescue Time (shows how you spend your PC time).

If distractions are a big issue for you, then I highly suggest setting up such contracts. Otherwise, you'll always find a way to rationalize your behavior. With a commitment contract, those rationalizations disappear immediately.

Chapter Summary

The idea: Distractions such as Facebook, TV programs, or video games are major enablers of procrastination. Research shows that the more enticing the distractions are, the more we procrastinate. Considering how attractive (downright addictive!) modern distractions are, it's no wonder so many of us are struggling with procrastination.

The tactics

Eliminate or Complicate: One problem with modern distractions is that they are too easily accessible. If we want to procrastinate less, we need to eliminate or complicate their access. We can do that by blocking distracting websites, deleting distracting apps on our smartphones, uninstalling computer games, or selling our game consoles.

Mold Your Environment: Everything in our environment has an unconscious impact on us. Some things trigger us to procrastinate, while others trigger us to work. We want to remove anything that could trigger procrastination from our environment and fill it instead with things that could trigger better productivity. Some common examples we've discussed are eliminating bookmarks, cleaning up your desktop, putting your phone in airplane mode, getting rid of notifications, and decluttering your work and living space.

Make Distractions Pay: By setting up commitment contracts (e.g., "I'll pay $500 every time I check Instagram before finishing my dissertation"), you make distractions a lot less attractive. In fact, you can make them so unappealing that not even the monkey wants anything to do with them.

Chapter 8

The Power of Nice — Why Self-Criticism Won't Get You Anywhere and What to Do Instead

Do you ever criticize yourself for being a procrastinator?

Do you make yourself feel bad if you fail to meet your perfectionistic standards?

Do you beat yourself up mentally after missing yet another deadline?

Welcome to the club! That's called self-criticism, and it's what most procrastinators are absolute pros at. In fact, it's something most people in today's society seem to be incredibly good at.

But does self-criticism really work? Does it do you any good? Does it help you get better?

Nope.

Most of us have engaged in self-criticism all of our lives... and if we are to believe the statistics on depression, suicide, happiness, and general well-being, this way of relating to ourselves hasn't exactly been a success.

In fact, recent research has shown that self-criticism is strongly related to depression and dissatisfaction with life. Self-critics are more likely to attempt suicide than others and experience more feelings of anxiety, shame, insignificance, and guilt. More surprisingly yet, research has shown that the constant criticism does *not* help individuals achieve more financial or material success. Ouch. Lots of negatives. No positives.

So, is there an alternative?

Indeed there is.

And it's one that is far superior to self-criticism.

According to the research, this alternative is a powerful way to achieve emotional well-being, stress resiliency, and even financial success. It has been shown that practicing this alternative helps people avoid destructive patterns of negativity, fear, and isolation while helping them experience more positive mental states such as optimism, hope, and happiness. Practitioners also benefit from better relationships and are more likely to achieve the goals they set for themselves.

Most critically for our discussion, this alternative has been shown to help people procrastinate less. But I'm getting ahead of myself.

So what's this mysterious alternative?

It's called *self-compassion*, and while it may not be the manliest of tactics, it's definitely one of the most powerful ones to have in your anti-procrastination arsenal.

In this chapter, we'll first discuss what self-compassion is, exactly. Then we'll look at why self-criticism leads to *more* procrastination while self-compassion leads to *less* procrastination. In the end, we'll discuss a practical approach you can use to make use of this life-changing information to curb your procrastination tendencies.

What Exactly Is Self-Compassion?

To understand self-compassion, we first need to understand compassion.

Compassion.com defines it as follows: "Compassion means 'to suffer with' and is an emotional response of sympathy. But it's not just a feeling. The feeling is combined with a desire to help. Because we have compassion, we want to take action and help the person who is suffering."

Compassion is a feeling that arises when you're confronted with someone else's suffering, combined with a desire or motivation to relieve that suffering.

From a biological standpoint, compassion results in a slowing down of our heart rate, secretion of the "bonding hormone" oxytocin, and activation of brain regions linked to caregiving, empathy, and feelings of pleasure. These biological changes result in our wanting to approach and care for the suffering being.

You may experience compassion when your daughter comes home with a bad grade, when you hear news of a disaster, when your spouse is struggling with a cold, or when your best friend just got divorced.

In each of these cases, you will likely feel warmth, sympathy, and the desire to help the suffering being in whatever way possible. You will treat the individual with love and kindness, rather than judgment.

Self-compassion involves acting the same way toward yourself when you're having a hard time, when you experience failure, or when you notice something you dislike about yourself.

Instead of ignoring or suppressing your suffering, you acknowledge it. Instead of criticizing yourself for your inadequacies and shortcomings, you comfort and care for yourself. You treat yourself with love, warmth, patience, and understanding.

Self-compassion means to recognize your own suffering and do your best to alleviate it.

For our purposes, we'll just look at self-compassion as the opposite of self-criticism. It's about treating ourselves like a nice person, rather than a lost cause. It's about forgiveness and understanding, rather than criticism and judgment.

Let's now discuss why self-criticism leads to more procrastination, and why self-compassion leads to less procrastination.

Why Self-Criticism Leads to Procrastination

Whenever I talk to people about self-compassion, they raise the notion that becoming more self-compassionate will somehow make them complacent and self-indulgent.

In reality, the opposite is true. But I see where that notion is coming from... Self-criticism *can* work as a motivator through the mechanism of fear.

Because it's so unpleasant to be harshly criticized by ourselves when we fail, we naturally want to avoid that. We become motivated by the desire to escape self-judgment. It's like a kid being motivated by the fear of getting beaten by his father. While self-judgment may not be physically painful, the emotional pain can often be immense.

The underlying thought process goes like this: "If I can't get myself to do this, then I'll get a terrible mental beating later on. I really need to force myself to do this, otherwise I'll feel guilty, disappointed, ashamed, and so on."

While this approach works to a certain extent, it comes with some serious drawbacks.

To begin with, those threats create heaps of stress and anxiety, both of which can severely impact performance. This is well-known as performance anxiety, which has been shown to be a performance-killer by distracting people from their task and interfering with their ability to focus. Contrary to popular belief, pressure does not improve performance, but rather undermines it.

In addition to that, self-criticism leads to a peculiar phenomenon called *self-handicapping*, a kind of self-sabotage designed to undermine performance in order to save face in case of failure. We tend to do that so that if we fail, we can avoid feeling unworthy by blaming failure on not having enough time, not trying hard enough, or not caring enough.

It's a behavior I used to engage in all the time during high school. You see, I always thought of myself as one of the smartest kids. And because I wanted to uphold that image, I couldn't risk studying hard for an exam and failing. After all, that would have meant I wasn't that smart, and frankly, my ego couldn't take that. So I self-handicapped by never properly studying for a test. Whenever I got a bad or average grade, I blamed it on my lack of studying. (Needless to say, this kind of self-sabotage didn't exactly help me reach my full potential.)

Procrastination, it turns out, is also a form of self-handicapping.

And guess what? Self-criticism tends to be the driving force behind it. Kristin Neff, a leading self-compassion and mindfulness researcher, explains the link in her book *Self-Compassion*:

"Research indicates that self-critics are less likely to achieve their goals because of these sorts of self-handicapping strategies. In one study, for instance, college students were asked to describe their various academic, social, and health-related goals, and then to report on how much progress they had made toward these goals. Self-critics made significantly less progress toward their goals than others and also reported that they procrastinated more often."

Self-critics make significantly less progress toward their goals and report procrastinating more often.

This finding goes hand-in-hand with another study I've recently come across in Kelly McGonigal's book *The Willpower Instinct*. She writes:

"Consider, for example, a study at Carleton University in Ottawa, Canada, that tracked the procrastination of students over an entire semester. Lots of students put off studying for the first exam, but not every student made it a habit. Students who were harder on themselves for procrastinating on their first exam were more likely to procrastinate on later exams than students who forgave themselves.

The harder they were on themselves about procrastinating the first time, the longer they procrastinated for the next exam! Forgiveness — not guilt — helped them get back on track."

This bears repeating: *the harder they were on themselves about procrastinating the first time, the longer they procrastinated for the next exam. Forgiveness — not guilt — helped them get back on track.*

If you want to keep your procrastination habit going, make sure to continually beat yourself up over any flaws and shortcomings you might have. Bring on the guilt and self-punishment, and harshly criticize yourself at every opportunity you get.

The point is this: Self-criticism leads to more procrastination.

Far from being a source of motivation, it only makes things worse and keeps adding fuel to your procrastination habit.

So, what about self-compassion?

Why Self-Compassion Leads to Less Procrastination

Research has shown over and over again that self-compassion increases motivation, performance, health, success, and almost any other aspect of life in multiple ways.

To keep things short here, we'll just focus on one way in which self-compassion increases productivity and reduces procrastination: reduced fear of failure.

Self-compassionate people experience far less fear of failure than their self-critical peers. They basically know that they'll be fine in spite of failure. They don't need to *fear* self-punishment because they don't *engage* in self-punishing behavior. When they fail, they forgive and console themselves. They build themselves back up. They support and encourage themselves.

Research shows that self-compassionate people see failure as something positive, as a learning opportunity. They simply take it as feedback, applaud themselves for trying, and get back on track.

For self-compassionate people, failing, taking risks, and getting on the playing field is something to be embraced, rather than feared. It's an opportunity for growth, not a measure of self-worth.

And because self-compassionate people don't fear failure, they're able to take more action and risks. They don't need to self-handicap because their self-worth isn't at risk in the first place. They're okay with who they are, and they don't equate their worthiness with their successes or failures.

Self-compassion creates a safe environment, allowing us to try out and risk things without being stressed and anxious about getting punished in case of failure. It basically allows you to operate from a place of confidence, calm, and security. When you operate from that place of safety, you're not as afraid of failure, and so there's no reason to self-sabotage and procrastinate to save your ego.

Oh, and this isn't just "feel-good talk." Kristin Neff presents rock-solid science proving that self-compassionate people procrastinate less than their self-critical peers in her book *Self-Compassion*.

My own experience fully supports these findings. Treating myself in a more compassionate way and forgiving myself for my mistakes (procrastination-related or otherwise) has made a huge difference in my life.

Back in my self-critical days, I'd wake up in the morning, already feeling a bit anxious about the day ahead. I was scared of what was going to happen if I didn't live up to my expectations. I knew that if I wasn't highly productive, I'd give myself a terrible mental beating and burden myself with a debilitating amount of guilt.

My emotional life was filled with anxiety, disappointment, shame, and guilt. Considering what we know about the impact of negative emotions, it's obvious why I kept procrastinating and couldn't get anything done. While I was wrestling with my negative self-talk, the monkey was running the show.

Self-compassion has freed me from a lot of these toxic emotions, and with that, it has made me a lot more productive.

For one thing, I'm no longer terribly afraid of having an unproductive day. I know that I'll be fine and can live with myself whether I'm as productive as I'd like to be or not.

Most importantly, self-compassion has almost completely eliminated the guilt I feel when catching myself procrastinating. Instead of wallowing in shame and self-pity, I now forgive myself and move on with life. I get back on track a lot more quickly and can perform from a space of safety and calm.

It's hard to put in words just how powerful self-compassion can be when overcoming procrastination.

Like I said, it's made a massive difference in my own life, and I highly suggest giving this a try in yours.

With that being said, how exactly can you harness the powers of self-compassion to overcome procrastination? Here's the one specific strategy I suggest you start using…

TRY THIS: Forgive Yourself

Our natural tendency is to get all self-critical after procrastinating.

We give ourselves a hard time, make ourselves feel terrible, and basically bathe ourselves in a soup of guilt, shame, disappointment, discouragement, self-pity, and other negative emotions.

Not only do these negative emotions feel terrible, they also make it almost impossible to get anything worthwhile done. Why? Because the monkey in our head can't stand the negativity and wants to numb itself by engaging in distractions like Facebook, TV, video games, or the like.

The moment you stop distracting yourself, you're exposed to the negative emotions and the whole nonsense begins all over again.

As we've discussed, beating yourself up after procrastinating only makes things worse.

What you need to do instead is forgive yourself.

Realize that procrastination inevitably happens from time to time.

That's okay. That's natural.

It happens to all of us. No need to get all worked up about it. You tried, you did your best, and it didn't work out this time. And of course, it's okay to feel a little bit guilty and dissatisfied. That's normal. Instead of suppressing these emotions, just let them be there. Resolve to do better next time.

If you want, you can even consider actively consoling yourself. Give yourself a bit of a hug. Give yourself a pep talk. Treat yourself like you would treat a good friend in the same situation.

The goal is to forgive yourself and build yourself back up.

This allows you to bring some positive emotions of warmth, care, and love into the picture. Slowly but surely, those positive emotions displace the negative ones and before you know it, the monkey has gone back into its cave and you're able to take effective action once again.

Chapter Summary

The idea: Research clearly shows that self-criticism leads to more procrastination while self-compassion leads to less procrastination. To overcome procrastination, stop unfairly criticizing yourself and instead treat yourself with warmth, love, kindness, and understanding.

Forgive Yourself: Each act of procrastination can be used to practice forgiveness and self-compassion. Next time you fall short of your lofty aspirations and are about to beat yourself up, stop and remember what we talked about here. Instead of giving yourself a mental beating, forgive yourself as best you can. Remember, it's natural to procrastinate from time to time. It's okay. We all do it. Human life is hard. It's okay to feel bad, guilty, sad, or whatever. That's also natural. Treat yourself like you would treat a good friend and resolve to do better next time.

Chapter 9

The Art of Emotion Surfing — How to Do What Needs to Get Done… No Matter What.

The more I observe procrastination in my life, the more I realize just how much it has to do with emotion management.

Whether we see it or not, it's always the same story.

1) We don't *feel* like doing the difficult thing.

2) We end up doing something else that *feels* better.

This tends to play out well below the level of our conscious awareness, covered up by reasonable sounding excuses and rationalizations of a pleasure-seeking monkey.

We've discussed this in chapter one, but it bears repeating: Procrastination is always, always, always the story of negative emotions getting in our way.

For starters, we procrastinate on tasks that inspire negative feelings in us — tasks that are boring, overwhelming, frustrating, important, or difficult.

Furthermore, we procrastinate the most when we're in a bad mood — when we're angry, sad, disappointed, or feeling guilty.

It doesn't matter where the negative emotions come from.

Once they're there, the monkey shows up and urges us to run away from what feels uncomfortable and toward immediate gratification. Before we know it, we've wasted another day satisfying the monkey's addiction to pleasure.

If we want to overcome procrastination, we need to get better at emotion management. We need to make a drastic change in our relationship with emotions and instead of being at their mercy, we need to get back in control.

In this chapter, we'll look at a fantastic way of doing that.

But first, a little more about emotions and their relationship to behavior.

Slaves of Our Emotions

Most people in our society tend to have a very childish, one-way relationship with feelings.

They feel a certain way and then act accordingly.

Feeling first. Behavior second.

When they feel angry, they lash out at others. When they feel anxious, they retreat. When they feel sad, they crawl into their bed. When they feel superior, they misconduct. When they feel inferior, they shut up.

It's as if they're just blindly taking orders.

Who cares if their commitments, values, or goals say otherwise? If they feel a certain way, they act it out without much of a second thought.

We keep preaching how much we value freedom in our society. Yet when it comes to our own behavior, we seem happy to act like slaves.

Ironic, isn't it?

Fortunately, it doesn't have to be that way. We don't have to act out whatever behavior our feelings invite us to. Feelings aren't destiny.

In scientific literature, feelings are said to exhibit something called an *action tendency*. When we feel angry, we have the tendency to clench our fists, shout, and lash out physically or verbally.

The key word here is *tendency*. We may *feel* like acting a certain way, but that doesn't mean we *have to* act that way. We can feel afraid, but act courageously. We can feel discouraged, but keep going. We can feel angry, but act calmly. We can feel like procrastinating, but perform the task anyway.

I'm sure you've experienced many examples of this in your own life. You may have felt tired and unmotivated, but still managed to finish your dissertation. You may have been afraid of asking that special someone out, but you found a way despite that.

The point is that while feelings undeniably *influence* your behavior, they shouldn't *dictate* it.

You can act a certain way, whether you feel like it or not. You can do what's right, important, or valuable, whether you feel like it or not.

This ability — doing what needs to get done regardless of how we're feeling — is the core of overcoming procrastination. The better we get at this skill, the less we will struggle with putting things off.

Why? Because ultimately, procrastination comes down to the all-important moment of facing a task, experiencing the pain and negative emotions associated with it, and then either running away or getting on with the task anyway.

Let's face it, the unfortunate truth is that certain tasks will always make us feel uncomfortable in some way. We will always feel like running away from what's difficult and toward what's easier.

We can't change that. If we strive to live a life of meaning, adventure, and growth, it's a given.

What we *can* change is our response.

We can stop blindly following our urges, impulses, and tendencies to act a certain way. We can become the type of person who follows through with their intentions, whether they're motivated or not.

We can get comfortable feeling uncomfortable. We can get things done in spite of experiencing fear, frustration, boredom, or being overwhelmed.

That's what it means to be a mature human being. David K. Reynolds puts it well in his book *Constructive Living*:

"The mature human being goes about doing what needs to be done regardless of whether that person feels great or terrible. Knowing that you are the kind of person with that kind of self-control brings all the satisfaction and confidence you will ever need. Even on days when the satisfaction and confidence just aren't there, you can get the job done anyway."

Once we understand the importance of this skill, it's time to face another truth.

It won't be as easy as I've made it sound.

Action tendencies of strong emotions are incredibly hard to resist — that's why so many of us are struggling with anger issues, depression, internet addiction, and of course, procrastination.

As far as procrastination is concerned, the action tendency is always the same: run away. Abandon the task and do something that feels better.

So far we've referred to this tendency as the monkey's pull toward immediate gratification. We've also briefly touched on it in chapter three — when we contemplate a difficult task, we literally feel pain, and because our natural response to pain is to run away, that's what we often do.

The question is, how can we handle this urge to run away — to procrastinate?

The strategy we're about to learn will help us. It's a mindfulness-based technique called *urge surfing* or *emotion surfing* and was originally discovered by Eastern traditions and religions, where it has been used for thousands of years.

Nowadays, it's a scientifically studied intervention that has successfully helped people overcome addictions, quell anxiety, relieve depression, reduce pain, bring about emotional stability, and much more.

This tactic has been an absolute game-changer in my life, and I'm positive it can do similar things for you as well. Please don't get put off by its simplicity.

TRY THIS: Surf Your Emotions

Let's say you come home from work and decide to write some more of your novel.

As soon as you contemplate the idea, you feel the action tendency to run away, the pull toward immediate gratification, the urge to procrastinate.

What now? How do you handle this? How do you prevent yourself from procrastinating?

The first, most crucial step is to stay put.

Don't react.

Don't move an inch.

Instead, slow down and watch what's happening. Observe the sensations in your body. You'll likely feel uncomfortable doing this. You may even experience some pain.

That's okay. It's normal.

After a minute or two, you'll realize that you're able to tolerate the negative emotions. You're not going to die. And nothing terrible is happening to you.

Even better, you'll make the marvelous discovery that the negative emotions lose some of their power over you. And the urge to run away? It's also losing some of its strength.

You see, urges are kind of like waves. A wave starts off small and builds gently. Then it gradually gathers speed and grows bigger. It keeps growing and moving forward until it reaches its peak, known as the crest. Once the wave has crested, it gradually subsides. Urges do the same thing. They start off small, slowly increase in size until they crest, and then subside.

If you are able to stay with an urge to procrastinate for just a few minutes, the strength of it will decrease quickly, making it much easier to handle.

Staying put and accepting negative emotions is often all it takes to beat procrastination. After a short while, the emotions will have lost most of their power, and you are able to take effective action in spite of them.

The key to making this strategy work is to accept the emotions just as they are. Don't try to suppress them, vent them, or otherwise change or get rid of them. Just accept them. Don't struggle. Just let them be there, watch them, and welcome them. Stay with the sensations, make peace with them until they dissolve, and then take action.

And that's it. That's the whole technique.

While it may sound simple and naïve, it's incredibly effective. Thousands of years of history and countless scientific studies don't lie. Give it a try and you'll discover it for yourself.

But first, know that there's a catch…

To be able to use this technique in the first place requires quite a bit of awareness.

You can't use it when you haven't realized that you are or have been procrastinating. When you go to bed at night and realize you should have been studying, it's too late.

This is a technique to be used on the battlefield, not in the aftermath. The technique requires that you become aware of your own procrastination before the battle is over and lost. The earlier, the better.

That's why awareness is so crucial.

Without it, you'll never get the chance to change your destiny. You can't even see what's going on. You just act out your autopilot tendencies and impulses. You're like the Hulk, who only realizes what damage he's done when Bruce Banner "wakes up" and it's already over.

Don't be like that. Live with awareness. The great Socrates once said, "The unaware life is not worth living."

Anthony De Mello goes one step further in his book *Awareness*, stating: "The unaware life is a mechanical life. It's not human, it's programmed, conditioned. We might as well be a stone, a block of wood."

Anyway, I know this may sound a bit philosophical, so let's get back to the practical applications for overcoming procrastination. Up next is an example that will illustrate the relationship between awareness and urge surfing and how it can help you beat procrastination.

Let's use an example we're all too familiar with: studying. Your upcoming exams are important, so you're really motivated. As you're making your way to your desk, however, you're experiencing weird sensations of tension, resistance, and anxiety. You feel a sudden urge to check your email, watch TV, clean the room, or do anything else but study. Unfortunately, you're not consciously aware that this is happening, and before you know it, you've been dillydallying for an hour. Whoopsie!

Suddenly you realize what just happened — you become aware of your procrastination. You still have enough time. No big deal.

Thankfully, your awareness is spot-on this time. You realize that you've given in to immediate gratification and forsaken your long-term goals. You realize that studying conjures up negative emotions in you and that you're feeling guilty for wasting an hour of your precious time. You also realize that you're still experiencing the urge to run away from studying and engage in something more enjoyable.

Even better, you remember the practice of urge surfing you've learnt in this book. Instead of letting your emotions get the better of you, you start slowing down. Your resist the urge to run away and simply stay put. You observe the negative emotions in you and experience your bodily sensations in a nonjudgmental way, without trying to change anything. You let everything just be as it is. It's all good. You're accepting that you're feeling this way right now.

After about 30 seconds, you remember how important your upcoming exams are. You also remember that you'll immediately feel better once you've actually started studying. Equipped with that knowledge, you make your way to your desk, sit down, and throw yourself at your studies.

Five minutes in, the negative feelings have evaporated almost completely. You start feeling better about yourself. You're motivated. The subject is actually quite interesting. After a while, you realize you're making great progress and start feeling even better about yourself, even more motivated to rock the upcoming exams.

And that's it.

That's a simple illustration of how you can combine awareness and urge surfing as a powerful intervention for overcoming procrastination.

It always works the same way. You need to become aware that you have been procrastinating or that you are about to procrastinate. Then you need to accept any negative feelings associated with the dreaded task. And then you need to take action and just get started in spite of those feelings.

Awareness and emotion surfing. That's all you theoretically need.

But because we're all suffering from a lack of awareness and a weak emotion surfing ability, we can also greatly benefit from all the other strategies discussed in this book.

Before we wrap this up, there's one last thing I want to address…

What About Thoughts?

So far, I've focused strictly on feelings. But what about thoughts?

Here's where they enter the picture. Whenever you experience negative emotions, your monkey starts creating one excuse after another designed to convince you to abandon future interests and give in to immediate gratification.

These excuses often sound superficially reasonable. In reality, however, they are all interchangeable, recurrent, and only serve the purpose of abandoning anything that's even remotely uncomfortable for something that feels better immediately.

Some of the most common excuses for procrastinating are:

- "I'll feel more like it tomorrow!"

- "I work better under pressure."

- "I'm too tired. I'll do it when I have more energy."

- "There's even more work after this. I can never get it all done."

- "Damnit! I should have started earlier. Now it's too late. I might as well give up."

- "I need some more preparation before I can start."

- "I'll feel more like doing it after another cup of coffee."

- "I'm too jittery to get work done. I shouldn't have drank that last cup of coffee."

- "It's already 4 p.m. Now it's too late to start. I'll just do it tomorrow."

- "Today is Sunday. It's okay to rest and do nothing. I'll just do it tomorrow."

- "I'm not motivated. Let me Google how to increase motivation."

- "I can't concentrate today. It would be a waste of time trying to get anything done."

Sound familiar?

When trying to overcome procrastination, it's best to just ignore these kinds of thoughts.

Don't take them so seriously. If you look closely, most thoughts are actually useless anyway — just the ramblings of a pleasure-addicted monkey.

"I'm too tired. Let's watch TV!"

"I don't feel like it. Let's go on Facebook!"

"This is boring. Let's play video games!"

Of course the monkey wants to watch TV, go on Facebook, and play video games. Of course it will tell you to abandon your dreams and aspirations of a better future. We can expect that.

Here's the secret: You don't need to listen to the monkey. You don't need to follow its orders.

Let the monkey cry itself out. Let it throw its tantrums. Let it revolt. What's the problem? You don't take orders from a spoiled child, do you?

Let the monkey do its thing. You do yours.

Just allow thoughts and emotions to be there. Accept them. Acknowledge them. And take effective action regardless.

Chapter Summary

The idea: We procrastinate because we don't *feel* like it. We let negative emotions get in the way and then follow our monkey's pull toward doing something that *feels* better. Overcoming procrastination is about realizing that we're not at the mercy of our thoughts and emotions. It's about realizing that we can do the right thing whether we feel like it or not. It's about learning to do the right thing no matter what.

The tactics

Surf Your Emotions: Next time you experience negative emotions and feel the urge to run toward immediate gratification, stop and slow down. Don't do anything. For 30-60 seconds, just stay put and observe your own thoughts and emotions. Just watch what's happening. Just feel the sensations in your body. Let the urge ride itself out. After about a minute or so, you'll find that the urge has lost much of his power. You're able to overcome those negative emotions and get started on the task.

Chapter 10

The Science of Willpower — Why It's the Secret to Overcoming Procrastination and Living a Healthy, Happy, and Successful Life

Procrastination can be defined as a form of willpower failure.

We can also call it self-regulation failure, self-control failure, self-discipline failure, or whatever-else-people-call-it failure.

The issue is that you *want* to study more, finish projects on time, get up earlier, or exercise regularly. The desire is there, but you can't get yourself to make these things happen. In other words, you fail to regulate your behavior.

Procrastination shares this fate with many other self-regulation problems, such as excessive gambling, overeating, drinking too much, and reckless spending.

The issue is always the same. The monkey is pulling you in all the wrong directions, but you lack the willpower to veto it.

More often than not, the reason we fail to regulate our behavior comes down to negative emotions. That's why the last chapter taught you a powerful skill to deal with negative emotions, helping you to better regulate your behavior in spite of them.

In this chapter, we're going to dive deeper into the science of self-regulation and willpower.

Since overcoming procrastination ultimately comes down to willpower — every time you resist the urge to procrastinate is an act of willpower — it is incredibly helpful to learn more about how it works and how to get better at it.

Any improvement in your overall self-control directly translates into less procrastination.

The better you get at willpower, the less you'll struggle with procrastination.

The good news is that willpower is very much subject to change. If you're willing to put in the necessary time and effort, you can strengthen your willpower significantly. In other words, you can become much more self-disciplined.

I can offer a great personal example. For most of my life, my self-discipline has been an utter and complete joke. I couldn't get myself to study for exams, I couldn't get up on time, I couldn't stop playing my favorite video game until 4 a.m., and I couldn't stop getting drunk every weekend. Heck, I could barely sign up for university classes on time!

Without a huge amount of outside pressure, I literally couldn't get myself to do anything, not even the simplest things like throwing away old milk cartons, cleaning dirty dishes, or washing my sweaty gym clothes that had been stinking up my room for weeks.

Looking back, I wonder how I ever got anything done at all.

Today, things look a whole lot better. My room is always orderly. I get up on time every day. I haven't used the snooze function on my phone in over a year. I'm meditating daily. I'm taking cold showers daily. I'm exercising multiple times a week. I read about 100 books a year. I eat healthy. I do the dishes right after eating or cooking. I pay my bills on time. And so on.

I'm not telling you that to impress you. I just want to show you that it's possible to go from almost zero self-control to a level that allows you to live a healthy, happy, and inspired life.

And don't get me wrong. I still struggle a lot.

But the number of unwelcome surprises, worried nights, and the frequency of crippling stress and anxiety I experienced along with procrastination have been drastically reduced.

So, what can you do to improve your self-control?

We'll get to that in a sec, but first, let's discuss some of the basics of willpower. Here's a quick Willpower 101 class.

What Exactly Is Willpower?

Over the years, people have defined willpower in many different ways. Some of the most common are:

- "The ability to get done what needs to get done, whether you feel like it or not."

- "The ability to delay gratification, resisting short-term temptations in order to meet long-term goals."

- "Conscious, effortful regulation of the self by the self."

- "The capacity to override an unwanted thought, feeling or impulse."

At its core, willpower is the skill of noticing what you are about to do and choosing to do the more difficult thing instead of the easiest. It's the skill of feeling the pull of the monkey toward immediate gratification and resisting it. It's the ability to resist short-term pleasure in favor of long-term success.

Why Is It So Important?

Willpower is the #1 predictor of happiness, health, wealth, and one's general "success" in life. Period.

According to Roy Baumeister, a leading researcher in this field, people with greater willpower are happier, healthier, and more satisfied in their relationships. They make more money and are further ahead in their careers. They are better able to manage stress, deal with conflict, and overcome adversity. They even live longer than their less disciplined peers.

Baumeister cites countless studies in his book *Willpower*, showing that willpower is a better predictor of academic achievement than intelligence, a stronger determinant of effective leadership than charisma, and more important for marital satisfaction than empathy.

He sums up the benefits nicely in his book: "…found that improving willpower is the surest way to a better life.

They've come to realize that most major problems, personal and social, center on failure of self-control: compulsive spending and borrowing, impulsive violence, underachievement in school, procrastination at work, alcohol and drug abuse, unhealthy diet, lack of exercise, chronic anxiety, explosive anger. Poor self-control correlates with just about every kind of individual trauma: losing friends, being fired, getting divorced, winding up in prison."

Improving your willpower is the single greatest thing you can do to improve your life.

And as far as procrastination goes, anything that improves your willpower will also help you better deal with procrastination.

The more willpower you have, the less you'll struggle with procrastination.

How Does It Work?

Psychologists often use the analogy of a muscle to explain how willpower works.

Just like a muscle, self-control gets fatigued with heavy use, and thus varies in strength from moment to moment. Even the world's strongest biceps get tired sometimes, and so does your willpower muscle.

One classic study of this theory is called the radish experiment. Roy Baumeister and his team presented hungry college students with a bowl of chocolates and a bowl of radishes.

Both bowls were placed in front of each student, who was then left alone sitting in front of the bowls. Half of the students were told to eat some of the chocolates and to not eat any of the radishes. The other half were asked to eat some of the radishes while avoiding the chocolates.

The researchers expected the radish-eaters to use up a significant amount of willpower. To find out if that was the case, the researchers gave each student a difficult — in fact, unsolvable — puzzle to solve. What interested the researchers was how long students would work on it before giving up.

Lo and behold, as the muscle theory would predict, the researchers found that the radish-eaters gave up much faster than the chocolate-eaters did. They had used up a lot of willpower resisting the chocolates and were left exhausted when trying to solve the puzzle.

This experiment has been replicated in different variations hundreds of times, and the results are always the same. If you've just finished doing something that requires a lot of willpower, you've spent a lot of your overall willpower strength as well. There's only so much willpower available in your tank. Once you've used it all up, you lose your ability to self-regulate on upcoming tasks.

You probably experience this in your life all the time. When you come home after a stressful day at work, what are you more likely to do: the easy thing or the hard thing? Watch TV or exercise?

With your willpower tank almost empty, it's pretty much impossible to veto the monkey's pull toward immediate gratification.

The radish and other experiments explain the first part of the muscle theory: willpower is like a muscle that gets fatigued with use.

But there's another aspect to the analogy. While a muscle becomes exhausted by exercise in the short-term, it's strengthened by regular exercise in the long-term. Likewise, regularly exerting self-control improves your overall willpower strength.

One of the first studies demonstrating this idea asked volunteers to follow a two-week regimen to track their food intake, improve their posture, or track their moods. Compared to a control group, the participants who had exerted willpower by performing these small exercises were less vulnerable to self-control depletion in follow-up lab tests.

Another study showed that students assigned to a daily exercise regimen not only improved their physical fitness, but also became less likely to waste their money on impulse purchases and were more likely to wash the dishes instead of leaving them in the sink.

Roy Baumeister, one of the world's leading researchers in the field of self-control, explains it well in his book *Willpower*:

"Exercising self-control in one area seemed to improve all areas of life. They smoked fewer cigarettes and drank less alcohol. They kept their homes cleaner. They washed dishes instead of leaving them stacked in the sink, and did their laundry more often. They procrastinated less. They did their work and chores instead of watching television or hanging out with friends first. They ate less junk food, replacing their bad eating habits with healthier ones."

Over and over again, research shows that engaging in activities that require self-control helps build your overall self-control muscle.

With all of that being said, let's discuss some of the best strategies to get better at self-control.

I purposefully use the term "get better at" because it's not only about strengthening your willpower; it's also about using it more wisely.

Oh, and be warned — strategies that are proven to grow your willpower muscle are, by definition, hard. You don't grow your biceps by lifting Styrofoam weights. Likewise, you don't grow your willpower by doing things that are easy.

If you want more self-control, you need to stretch beyond your current level — and that's hard!

TRY THIS: Optimize Your Health and Energy Levels

Want to know the #1 reason people give for procrastinating?

According to Dr. Piers Steel, a leading procrastination researcher, it's fatigue. He writes in his book *The Procrastination Equation*:

"Whether tiredness is drug-induced or not, being too tired is the number-one reason given for procrastinating; 28 percent of people claim, 'Didn't have enough energy to begin the task' as the cause... Fatigue increases task-aversion, saps interest, and makes the difficult excruciating."

The reason fatigue plays such a huge role is because the use of willpower, just like the use of any other muscle, takes energy.

That's right. Every act of willpower requires and uses up energy.

If you resist eating a piece of cake, that takes energy. If you suppress an emotion, like anger or laughter, that takes energy. If you cook a healthy dinner in spite of not feeling like it, that takes energy.

Interestingly enough, the energetic component for the willpower muscle is the same as for any other muscle: blood sugar. Researchers have found that if people perform a self-control task (e.g., ignoring distractions or controlling emotions), their blood sugar levels tend to drop. And the more a person's blood sugar level drops after a self-control task, the worse he or she performs on the next task.

If you give willpower-drained individuals a glass of lemonade, the resulting boost in their blood sugar temporarily restores willpower.

Blood sugar problems (which translate into unstable and generally low energy levels) predict a wide range of willpower failures. Both diabetics and hypoglycemics are struggling to resist their impulses and delay gratification.

Roy Baumeister writes about both cases in his book *Willpower*:

"The link between glucose and self-control appeared in studies of people with hypoglycemia, the tendency to have low blood sugar. Researchers noted that hypoglycemics were more likely than the average person to have trouble concentrating and controlling their negative emotions when provoked. Overall, they tended to be more anxious and less happy than average. Hypoglycemia was also reported to be unusually prevalent among criminals and other violent persons, and some creative defense attorneys brought the low-blood-sugar research into court."

He goes on to mention a study that found below-average glucose levels in 90% (!) of juvenile delinquents taken into custody.

All in all, people with hypoglycemia are more likely to be convicted of a wide range of offenses: shoplifting, public profanity, destruction of property, traffic violations, intimate partner violence, child abuse, public masturbation, and so on.

Low blood sugar levels translate into low energy. And low energy levels mean these people have trouble regulating their behavior, resulting in more crime and other self-control-related issues.

The same thing seems to happen with diabetics. (While they have high blood sugar levels, their bodies have trouble converting that blood sugar into energy, which also results in a lack of available energy.)

"Researchers testing personality have found that diabetics tend to be more impulsive and have more explosive temperaments than other people their age. They're more likely to get distracted while working on a time-consuming task. They have more problems with alcohol abuse, anxiety, and depression. In hospitals and other institutions, diabetics throw more tantrums than other patients. In everyday life, stressful conditions seem to be harder on diabetics. Coping with stress typically takes self-control, and that's difficult if your body isn't providing your brain with enough fuel."

I've gotten a bit sidetracked here, but the point is that self-control requires energy.

If you don't have energy, you don't have self-control. Or as Roy Baumeister puts it: no glucose, no willpower.

It's that simple.

It doesn't even matter where your lack of energy is coming from — whether you've just had a tough day at work, eaten too much energy-draining junk food, consumed too much alcohol, have blood sugar issues, have adrenal issues, eaten too much food in general, or just have had a bad night's sleep.

If you lack energy, you won't be able to withstand the monkey's constant pulls toward immediate gratification.

If you want to overcome procrastination, you need a good and stable supply of energy. In fact, I would go as far as saying that the more energy you have, the less you'll struggle with procrastination.

Let me repeat that: The more energy you have, the less you'll struggle with procrastination.

Anything you can do to improve your health and energy levels will help you overcome procrastination. There's another reason to eat healthy and mind your health!

The implications of this truth are rather obvious. If you're chronically sleep-deprived, stressed out, drinking too much alcohol, and stuffing yourself with junk food, you need to re-consider your lifestyle.

If you're serious about overcoming procrastination, you need to get serious about your health and energy as well.

For starters, get enough sleep, optimize your diet, and exercise regularly.

In addition to that, I highly suggest investing some of your time and money into learning more about good sleep, proper nutrition, and exercise. I can tell you from my own experience that improving my sleep, nutrition, exercise, and other health-related aspects of my life has been absolutely game-changing for me.

When I drink too much alcohol, sleep too little, or eat too much crappy food, my procrastination rises dramatically. It's so much harder to overcome resistance when I'm feeling tired.

Unfortunately, I don't have time to go into any specific health-related recommendations here. I can, however, point you in the right direction.

If you wish to learn more about optimizing your health and energy levels, I suggest checking out the following people's websites, books, and other resources: Dave Asprey, Mark Sisson, Ben Greenfield, Dr. David Perlmutter, Dr. Mark Hyman, Dr. Mercola, and Katy Bowman.

These are some of my go-to resources when it comes to living a healthy and high-powered lifestyle.

TRY THIS: Simplify Your Life

Making decisions is hard work.

Depending on the type of decision, you must consider possible upsides and downsides, take responsibility, struggle with moral questions, and so on. It's an energy-intensive process that leads to a peculiar phenomenon called *decision fatigue*: The more decisions you make, the worse your judgment becomes.

Every decision you make takes energy. And unfortunately for you and me, that's the same energy we're using for willpower as well. Every decision you make sucks a little bit of fuel out of your willpower tank. The harder the decision, the more energy/willpower will be needed.

When you start your day, the tank is full (provided you've had a good night's sleep!). Every time you exert effort, you withdraw a bit of fuel, slowly emptying your tank. Choosing what to eat for breakfast drains a little bit. Same with deciding what to wear. Same with deciding whether to hit the gym before work or not.

Marketing experts have known about decision fatigue for years. That's why they put candy and other brightly packaged goodies at registers. As you make decisions while shopping, your blood sugar dips. By the time you're ready to check out, you're more likely to crave sugar to replenish your blood sugar stores than you were when you came in the door.

The good news is you can reduce the number of decisions you make, helping you save your precious willpower to beat procrastination and put toward something else important to you.

Here are three simple things you can do to reduce decision fatigue and free up willpower.

Plan your day the night before. What clothes am I going to wear today? What should I eat for breakfast? Should I hit the gym or sleep for another half hour? These are decisions that can be made the night before, which means you won't be wasting your self-control on those choices the next day.

Eat the same meals over and over again. I have the same breakfast every day — a black coffee. For lunch, it's (almost) always a combination of steamed veggies and cheese or a piece of meat. For dinner, it's a decision between three meals I cycle through. Very few decisions, right? Now compare that to the average person who's been shown to make 226 decisions about food per day.

Minimize your wardrobe. Steve Jobs was famous for his sneakers and black turtleneck. Barack Obama cycled through the same three or four suits during his presidency. Mark Zuckerberg has 10 identical gray shirts in his closet. You don't need to go that far, but try to simplify your wardrobe a bit. The less stuff you've got in there, the fewer decisions your brain is forced to make.

As a general guideline, anything that helps you simplify your life will help reduce decision fatigue and keep more willpower in your tank to beat procrastination.

TRY THIS: Meditate

Neuroplasticity is a term used to describe the brain's ability to change itself.

That's right, it turns out that the brain is incredibly responsive to experience and changes itself based on what you do. When you practice a certain behavior, you're strengthening the neural circuits responsible for that behavior, making it more accessible and more likely to occur in the future.

When you're angry, you're literally getting better at being angry and the brain region associated with being angry will grow denser. When you're happy, you're getting better at being happy and the brain region associated with being happy will grow denser.

Just like that, you can train your brain to be better at self-control. And meditation is one of the best ways to do that.

Why? Because meditation has powerful effects on many skills related to willpower: focus, attention, impulse control, self-awareness, stress management, emotion regulation, and so on.

Regular meditators aren't just better at these things — they literally have their brains to show for it. They have more gray matter in the pre-frontal cortex (the area of the brain where willpower resides), as well as regions of the brain that support self-awareness.

And contrary to what you may think, it doesn't take years of practice to reap the benefits. Kelly McGonigal, an expert on all things willpower-related, says that a mere three hours of practice are enough to boost self-control. She writes in her book *The Willpower Instinct*:

"One study found that just three hours of meditation practice led to improved attention and self-control. After eleven hours, researchers could see those changes in the brain. The new meditators had increased neural connections between regions of the brain important for staying focused, ignoring distractions, and controlling impulses. Another study found that eight weeks of daily meditation practice led to increased self-awareness in everyday life, as well as increased gray matter in corresponding areas of the brain. It may seem incredible that our brains can reshape themselves so quickly, but meditation increases blood flow to the prefrontal cortex, in much the same way that lifting weights increases blood flow to your muscles. The brain appears to adapt to exercise in the same way that muscles do, getting both bigger and faster in order to get better at what you ask of it."

She says that the brains of meditators become finely tuned willpower machines over time.

If you want to improve your willpower with meditation, I suggest downloading an app called Headspace and taking their free 10-day challenge. The app teaches you mindfulness meditation (the type of meditation used in most of the studies) in an easy step-by-step fashion. It's the simplest way to start meditating and make it a daily practice that I've found.

TRY THIS: Exercise

Exercise is one of the absolute best tools you can use to strengthen your willpower.

Kelly McGonigal, the willpower expert I've mentioned, explains in *The Willpower Instinct*:

"Exercise turns out to be the closest thing to a wonder drug that self-control scientists have discovered. For starters, the willpower benefits of exercise are immediate. 15 minutes on a treadmill reduces cravings, as seen when researchers try to tempt dieters with chocolate and smokers with cigarettes. The long-term effects of exercise are even more impressive. It not only relieves ordinary, everyday stress, but it's as powerful an antidepressant as Prozac. Working out also enhances the biology of self-control by increasing baseline heart rate variability and training the brain. When neuroscientists have peered inside the brains of new exercisers, they have seen increases in both gray matter — brain cells — and white matter, the insulation on brain cells that helps them communicate quickly and efficiently with each other. Physical exercise — like meditation — makes your brain bigger and faster, and the prefrontal cortex shows the largest training effect."

The immediate question this quote provokes is: How much do I need to do?

The right answer depends on how much you're willing to do. Setting unrealistic goals that you're going to abandon in a week makes no sense. Besides that, there's no scientific consensus about how much exercise you need to do.

It's best to start with a modest and realistic goal — consistency over intensity is the maxim.

Anything that you like to do and gets you moving is great.

Best of all, walking, gardening, grocery shopping, yoga, swimming, dancing, playing with your kids or pets — they all count!

TRY THIS: Grow Your Self-Compassion

Self-compassion, the practice we discussed in chapter eight, is another great way to boost self-control.

Here's a short and concise explanation from Kelly McGonigal in *The Willpower Instinct*:

"If you think that the key to greater willpower is being harder on yourself, you are not alone. But you are wrong. Study after study shows that self-criticism is consistently associated with less motivation and worse self-control. It is also one of the single biggest predictors of depression, which drains both "I will" power and "I want" power. In contrast, self-compassion — being supportive and kind to yourself, especially in the face of stress and failure — is associated with more motivation and better self-control."

Remember the study on self-forgiveness versus self-criticism we talked about in the self-compassion chapter?

The more self-critical participants were in response to procrastinating the first time, the longer they procrastinated for the next exam. It's forgiveness, not guilt, which maximizes self-control and performance.

Like I mentioned previously, becoming more self-compassionate has made a huge difference in my life. Not only does it help me procrastinate less, but it makes me happier, healthier, and more successful in general.

Ultimately, it comes down to the question of how you want to coach yourself.

Think about it. If you could pick a coach who follows you 24/7 for the rest of your life, who would you pick?

The guy who criticizes you all the time, puts you down, makes you small, beats you up mentally, punishes you, and rules with a demoralizing whip? Or the guy who looks out for you, cares for you, treats you with respect, has your best interests in mind, picks you up when you're feeling down, and motivates you?

If you want to be a good coach for yourself and overcome procrastination along the way, leave self-criticism behind and choose the path of self-compassion.

The good news is, no matter how self-critical you currently are, you can change it.

Self-compassion, just like willpower, is a muscle. The more you train it, the better you get at it.

The best way to grow your self-compassion muscle is simply to use it regularly. Every time you're not feeling so well is a chance to practice compassion for yourself — maybe you're feeling angry, lonely, depressed, sad, or disappointed. In such a moment of suffering, treat yourself like you would treat a good friend: with love, warmth, and care.

Realize it's okay to feel this way and that other people feel this way too. It's normal to be imperfect and struggle from time to time. Realize also that any thoughts and emotions are impermanent; they come and go like clouds in the sky. See if you can simply watch your inner world as a compassionate, nonjudgmental observer.

You can even try to console and comfort yourself by talking to yourself in a kind, sympathetic, and understanding way. If you feel like it, you can give yourself a hug, gently stroke your arms, or lay your hands on your heart.

I know it sounds a bit silly at first, but give it a try.

What have you got to lose? It's not like other people are watching — they're too busy struggling with their own issues!

And if you want to learn more about the science of self-compassion, check out Kristin Neff's similarly titled book.

Above All, Practice, Practice, Practice

Self-control is a skill like any other. If you want to get better at it, you need to practice.

You see, the secret to superhuman willpower is willpower itself: self-discipline begets self-discipline. Every time you act with discipline, you grow that muscle and become a little bit more disciplined.

Every time you resist the cookie, you grow your willpower. Every time you opt for a book instead of the TV, you grow your willpower. Every time you resist the urge to check Facebook, you grow your willpower. Every time you get up early and resist hitting the snooze button, you grow your willpower. Every time you prioritize sleep over watching another episode of your favorite TV show, you grow your willpower.

And remember, growing your willpower muscle directly translates into procrastinating less.

Before we wrap up this chapter, there are two things I would like you to keep in mind on your journey to having more self-control.

First of all, start small. Don't try to go from zero to hero. Don't aim to get up early, go for a morning run, take a cold shower, and then meditate for 20 minutes. Unless you're already very disciplined, this is a recipe for failure, discouragement, and self-criticism.

Instead, start small. Slowly cut back on negative habits. Slowly build your life around positive, willpower-supporting habits. If you do that, you'll find your self-control steadily becoming stronger and stronger.

Second, expect lots of setbacks and drama on your journey.

You'll inevitably experience periods of despair, disappointment, and discouragement. You'll feel like nothing's working and you're moving backwards instead of forwards. You'll start doubting yourself. You'll fall back into old habits. And so on and so forth.

That's to be expected. The best thing you can do during those times is to work on your self-compassion.

Above all, stay patient. Building self-control takes time. Just keep at it and you'll be sure to reap the rewards.

Chapter Summary

The idea: Procrastination can be described as a self-control failure. If you want to do one thing, but end up doing something else, you simply lacked the necessary willpower to resist the allure of immediate gratification. In other words, you failed to control the self — you failed to control your own behavior. The good news is that willpower is subject to change. Even better, every improvement in willpower translates directly into an improvement with procrastination.

The tactics

Optimize your health and energy levels: Willpower is surprisingly physical and uses up the same energy we use for breathing, exercising, talking, moving around, etc. If your health sucks, you'll lack the energy required for willpower and you'll fail to overcome procrastination. The more energy you have, the more willpower you have, and the better you are at resisting the monkey's constant pulls toward immediate gratification. I suggest optimizing your nutrition, exercise, sleep, and other health habits.

Simplify your life: Every decision you make burns up a little bit of willpower — willpower that could be used to battle procrastination. By simplifying your life, you reduce the amount of decisions you have to make every day. Start by minimizing your wardrobe, planning your days the night before, and cycling through the same healthy meals over and over again.

Meditate: Meditation has been shown to be one of the best strategies to improve willpower and grow the correlating brain structures. I suggest starting a daily mindfulness meditation habit with the use of the Headspace app.

Exercise: Regular exercise is another powerful self-control booster. You don't even need to go to the gym — anything from gardening to playing with kids or pets counts! As a general guideline, you want to exercise intensively a couple of times per week and move at a low pace throughout the day as much as possible.

Grow your self-compassion: Self-compassion is one of my best kept secrets. It helps me cope with procrastination, makes me happier, relieves a lot of guilt, and has even been shown to boost willpower. From now on, resolve to treat yourself with understanding, care, and respect. Leave the constant criticism and harsh judgments behind. They only make things worse.

Final Thoughts

Well, there you have it.

Congrats on making it all the way to the end of this book. For a (soon to be ex-) procrastinator, that's a monumental task.

Hopefully, you've had a good time and learned a thing or two about procrastination. My hope is you'll be able to take action from the tips, strategies, and insights we've discussed.

Because that's the key right there — taking action.

You can read all the books in the world and learn fantastic ideas and tactics, but they won't create any meaningful change unless you apply them to your own life.

Unless you get your feet wet, nothing's going to change. Taking the leap from theory to practice, from knowing to doing, is what separates stagnation from growth and winners from dreamers.

One of my all-time favorite quotes illustrates this point beautifully. It's from *The Kybalion*:

"The possession of Knowledge, unless accompanied by a manifestation and expression in Action, is like the hoarding of precious metals — a vain and foolish thing. Knowledge, like wealth, is intended for Use. The Law of Use is Universal, and he who violates it suffers by reason of his conflict with natural forces."

Knowledge is intended for use — not applying it is a vain and foolish thing to do.

I feel this message is more appropriate at the end of a book on procrastination than anywhere else.

The typical reader, upon finishing the book, will say to themselves something along the lines of, "Wow, that was helpful information. I'll definitely apply it once I have the time."

Don't fall into that trap.

Start executing some of the tactics immediately upon closing this book.

Set some implementation intentions. Install a website-blocking browser extension. Declutter your desktop. Clean your room. Download the Headspace app.

Once you've implemented one strategy, you're 10x more likely to implement another, and another, and another. But you need to start somewhere, and you need to stop worrying about getting it perfect.

There's no perfect anti-procrastination regimen. Don't let your monkey tell you there is. It is just trying to make excuses for not taking action right now. The last thing the monkey wants to do right now is implement these tactics. Instead, it wants to watch some TV or hop on Facebook. "You deserve it," it will say.

Heck, you're probably already feeling a little anxious, tense, or insecure right now. You probably feel the urge to run away from taking action.

Don't do it.

Stay put. Relax. Then execute.

Oh, and one last piece of advice before we wrap this up: Be prepared for a bumpy ride. Overcoming procrastination isn't exactly a walk in the park. It's more like a never-ending pain in the ass.

It's hard work. It's messy. It's discouraging at times.

You'll experience many defeats on your road to redemption. You'll feel like you're not making enough progress. You'll feel like you're moving backwards. You'll feel like giving up and choosing comfort over growth.

That's normal.

Your job is to persevere. Forgive yourself for fucking up and get back on track as swiftly as possible.

The Buddha allegedly said, "Persevere in your quest and you will find what you seek. Pursue your aim unswervingly and you will gain victory. Struggle earnestly and you will triumph."

Just keep putting in the work and you *will* reap the rewards.

Best of luck on your journey.

—Nils Salzgeber

P.S. Speaking of Taking Action…

If you haven't already, now is the time to d0wnload the Action Guide.

To download, go here: njlifehacks.com/lp/procrastination-action-guide/

Downloading the Action Guide and doing the exercises will do more for overcoming procrastination than merely reading the book.

Why? Because you're forced to do something with the ideas presented here.

So far, this has been a passive process. The Action Guide forces you to become active – to reflect, think, plan, and prepare. This will make a massive difference in cementing these ideas firmly in your mind, which ensures you'll know exactly what to do when the urge to procrastinate strikes in real life.

Oh, and don't hesitate to drop me a message at nils@njlifehacks.com if you have any thoughts, questions, or feedback. I love hearing from readers, and I'll get back to you as soon as possible.

To a productive and prosperous life!

Thank You

Before the two of us part ways, I'd like to say thank you for purchasing and reading my guide.

I'm aware that you could have chosen any other book on the subject of procrastination, and I'm thrilled you chose this one.

So thanks for downloading my book and reading all the way to the end.

Now I'd like to ask for a small favor. Could you take a moment to leave a review for this book on Amazon?

I'd love to hear your feedback. This is my first book, and I'm curious to know if it's any good.

Thanks so much!

About the Author

Hey, I'm Nils.

And yes, this is a first-person author bio.

And no, I haven't got any fancy degrees or other astonishing accomplishments to brag about here.

Frankly, I'm just a regular guy (much like you, I suppose) looking to make the most out of my life. My goal is simple: I want to live a great life (again, much like you, I suppose).

The question is, how do we get there?

My answer is... drum roll, please... through continuous and rigorous self-improvement.

If we want to achieve our greatest potential, we need to invest in ourselves. We need to take risks, work hard, learn, learn, learn, and get a tiny bit better every single day.

I've been on this journey for a while now, and I'm learning a lot.

For a little over a year, I've been sharing my latest and greatest insights on mine and my brother Jonas' website at www.njlifehacks.com.

We write about productivity, procrastination, Stoicism, mindset, habits, and anything else that helps us live better.

If you're into this kind of stuff, subscribe to our newsletter to get exclusive material, updates, and more. We'd love to have you on board!

That's it from me.

To a productive and prosperous life,

—Nils Salzgeber

P.S.: Got questions or feedback? I'd love to hear about it. Just send me an email at: nils@njlifehacks.com.

Printed in Great Britain
by Amazon